Directory of *HISTORIC RACING CARS*

Directory of
HISTORIC
RACING
CARS

The Survivors - Genuine,
Authentic & Facsimile

Denis Jenkinson

Aston Publications

Published in 1987 by Aston Publications
Limited,
Bourne End House, Harvest Hill,
Bourne End, Bucks., SL8 5JJ

© Copyright Denis Jenkinson 1987

Note: All photographs in this book credited to
T. C. March are the copyright of Aston
Publications Limited.

ISBN 0 946627 08 8

Designed by Chris Hand

Photoset and printed in England by
Redwood Burn Limited,
Trowbridge, Wiltshire

Sole distributors to the
UK book trade,
Springfield Books Ltd.,
Norman Road, Denby Dale,
Huddersfield, West Yorkshire,
HD8 8TH.

Sole distributors in the United States,
Motorbooks International,
P.O. Box 2,
729 Prospect Avenue,
Osceola,
Wisconsin 54020,
United States.

Contents

Introduction

It would be asking too much to include every known racing car in a directory such as this, but a good cross-section has been included, especially of those that are still seen in action long after they have passed their prime. Racing cars are essentially built for a particular purpose and it was the normal way of things for them to be discarded after they had served that purpose. Some were able to be used in other forms of racing at a lower level, others could be used as road-going sports cars, while many remained in the state in which they were last raced and put on display by the parent factory or constructor. Some were simply broken up and destroyed once they had served their purpose.

The phenomenon of racing old cars was started by the Vintage Sports Car Club in 1936 and has proliferated ever since, developing into multitudinous categories all under the general term 'Historic'. Such has been the enthusiasm for racing old cars that it has been an almost impossible task to control, and brand new cars are being built specifically to be raced in Historic events! Historic cars or Historic events imply the possession of some history and not all the cars presented as Historic can actually claim any part of history, which has caused some confusion.

The building of a brand new car to an old design and claiming a piece of known history for it is basically fraudulent, although in most cases this is not done intentionally. So many people want to race an old *Alfabugaserati*, and there are insufficient to go round, that new ones are made. They cannot honestly take part in Historic events, so various subterfuges are indulged in, and if the guile of the owner is good enough, few people will know, and we arrive at the absurd situation of a brand new car winning an event of historic importance, as happened in the VSCC world in 1986.

As the years go by some of these fake cars are becoming old enough to establish their own history! If a genuine old car can show a continuous history of 50 years, where do we stand with one that has a 10-year continuous history, having been built as a 'Facsimile' in 1977. Is it now a genuine fake? – a car with proven provenance, identical to the one from which it was copied, except for a time span of 40 years.

The racing car scene has always been complicated because there has never been an official registry of racing cars, as there is with aircraft, and with the proliferation of old car activity the scene has become even more complex, hindered rather than helped by over-enthusiastic owners or unscrupulous owners or constructors.

The whole gamut of old racing cars is really only a hobby or pastime of no intrinsic significance or importance, but it has created a cottage industry within its ranks in which 'fakers' and 'fettlers' have been able to make an honest, or dishonest, living depending on their ethics.

In this book an attempt has been made to sort out the real from the unreal in order to try to retain a sense of proportion. If people want to take part in or witness 'Historic events' then a sense of history must be maintained. If they would be content to take part in racing 'for cars built in the old-style' there would be no problems. If that was to happen, then someone might begin to wonder why they do not build cars in the new-style and join in normal racing. The majority of people in the old-racing-car game are involved for sentimental reasons, such as the pleasure they get from driving the self-same racing car that their boyhood hero drove. If Nuvolari was your boyhood hero and you can now drive one of the Alfa Romeos that he raced, there can be no greater satisfaction. Equally your hero may have been Fangio, and your aim is to drive one of the Maseratis that he raced; or it could be a keen amateur who raced an M.G., and you are in that self-same M.G. indulging in Historic racing. It all makes good sense. To race a brand new car built in the old style seems a pointless exercise in comparison.

The cars dealt with in this book range from special factory Grand Prix cars, only ever driven by factory-employed drivers, to one-off home-made specials; but all were built for the express purpose of racing, whether in an International Grand Prix or a local speed trial. They cover the period that stretches roughly from 1920 to 1960, from the beginnings of the development of the classic Grand Prix car to the beginning of the 'new look' period of racing which was the true post-war modern racing car era.

Various clubs and bodies who organize old-car racing have their own definitions of what is historic, even last year's obsolete Grand Prix car is 'historic' in some people's eyes, but as a generalization we have taken historic to mean cars with the engines at the front. For fairly obvious reasons, some makes of car are dealt with in great detail, as regards individual cars, others have been dealt with in a more general way. Examples of most of the cars referred to can be seen in action in some form of competition, while others can be seen in museums or private collections. Some still exist, but are untraceable at the time of writing, and many are still moving about the busy old-car market place. For this reason owners' names have been omitted in many cases, for the car would be likely to have a new owner by the time this book was published.

Crondall, Hampshire, 1987   Denis Jenkinson

Glossary of Terms

'Original'

Almost impossible to find anything in this category. It would have had to have been put in store the moment it was completed. Possibly the Trossi-Monaco special in the Biscaretti Museum comes as close to an original racing car as it is possible to get.

The 'old-car industry' frequently uses degrees of originality, such as 'nearly original', 'almost original', even 'completely original', but all such descriptions are meaningless as they cannot be quantified. A racing car that has only had a new set of tyres and a change of sparking plugs since it was completed is no longer 'original'. Many components have remained 'original', such as gearboxes, cylinder heads, axles and so on, and reproduction parts are made to 'original drawings' and 'original material specification', but this does not make them 'original' parts, nor does a complete car built from such components qualify as 'original', regardless of what the constructor or owner might think. Such a car is nothing more than a 'reproduction' or 'facsimile'.

'Genuine'

This is a much more practical description for an old or historic car and can be applied to most racing cars that have had active and continuous lives, with no occasions when they 'disappeared into limbo' or changed their character in any way. Most E.R.A.s come into this category as they have been raced continuously, which has meant the replacing of numerous components as they wore out, but the car itself has never been lost from view, nor has its basic character and purpose been altered over the years. Even such a well-known E.R.A. as *'Romulus'* is not 'original', as it has been repainted, re-upholstered, new tyres have been fitted and new components have been used to rebuild the engine; but it is unquestionably 'Genuine'.

'Authentic'

This term is used to describe a racing car that has led a chequered career, through no fault of its own, but has never disappeared from view. The 'Entity', which is best described as the sum of the parts, has always been around in some form or other, but has now been put back to the specification that it was in, either when it was first built, or some subsequent known point in its history. An example would be an old Grand Prix car that was converted into a road-going sports car when its useful racing life was over, over the years having the racing engine replaced by a touring version, and eventually being allowed to deteriorate. It is then rescued and rebuilt as the Grand Prix car, with its racing engine replaced, but with new radiator, fuel tank and oil tank, new wheels made, new bodywork, instrument panel, seat, upholstery and so on, all of which were missing. The 'Entity' that started life as the Grand

Prix car never actually disappeared, so the end result of all the labours can justifiably be described as 'Authentic'. There is no question of it being 'Original', and to describe it as genuine would be unfair to its sister cars that remained Grand Prix cars all their lives, even though such things as radiator, fuel tank, seat and so on had to be replaced due to the ravages of time and use.

'Resurrection'

Some racing cars, when they reached the end of their useful life, were abandoned and gradually dismantled as useful bits were taken off to use on other cars. Eventually insufficient of the car remained to form an acceptable entity, even though most of the components were still scattered about. There have been numerous cases where such components that still existed were gathered up to form the basis of a new car; a new chassis frame and new body were required and, from the bare bones or the ashes of the original, another one appears. It cannot claim to be the original car, and certainly not a genuine car, nor an authentic car. At best it is a 'Resurrection' from the dead, or from the graveyard.

'Re-construction'

This can stem from a single original component, or a collection of components from a variety of cars, but usually there is very little left of the original racing car, except its history and its character. From these small particles a complete new car is built, its only connection with the original car being a few components and the last-known pile of rust left over when decomposition set in.

'Facsimile'

Purely and simply a racing car that now exists when there never was an original. If a factory built four examples of a particular Grand Prix model, for instance, and there are now five

George Abecassis with the Grand Prix Alta. (Guy Griffiths)

in existence, then the fifth can only be a facsimile, fake, clone, copy or reproduction. If the fifth car was built by the same people or factory who built the four original cars, then at best it could be a 'Replica' of the four genuine cars, but such a situation is very unlikely. There are many reasons for building a facsimile, from sheer enthusiasm for a particular model to simple avarice, and it is remarkable how many facsimiles have been given a small piece of genuine history in order to try to authenticate the fake, and thus raise its value.

Facsimiles have been built of just about everything from Austin to Wolseley, some being so well made that it is difficult to tell them from originals. Some owners have been known to remain strangely silent about the origins of their cars when they have been mistaken for the real thing. Other facsimiles have been declared openly and honestly by the constructors, such as the facsimile that has been built of an A/B-type E.R.A., or the series of facsimiles of 250F Maseratis that have been built. The trouble usually starts when the cars are sold to

A magnificent photograph of Juan Fangio with the Tipo 159 Alfa Romeo on his way to second place in the 1951 British Grand Prix. Until recently all the Tipo 159s were retained by the factory and are 'Genuine.' (Guy Griffiths)

The short wheelbase W196 of Juan Fangio in the 1955 Monaco Grand Prix. (LAT)

less scrupulous owners, who first convince themselves they have bought a genuine car, and then try to convince the rest of the sporting world. The disease is very prevalent in the world of museums, on the assumption that the paying public are gullible.

'Special'

This name applies to one-off cars that are the product of the fertile brain of the constructor. It is probably true to say that no special has ever been finished! It may be finished sufficiently to allow it to race, but inevitably the constructor will be planning further modifications while he is racing it. If the special builder ever says his car is finished, it will usually indicate that it is now obsolete and he is starting on a new one. The rebuilding or restoring of a special to use as an Historic racing car, by someone who is not the original constructor, can mean either that the car is rebuilt to a known point in time that appeals to the new owner, or he can continue the process of development where the originator left off.

The nice thing about specials is that they are a law unto themselves and do not need to be put into any sort of category. A special can be totally accepted as 'Genuine, authentic, reconstructed or facsimile'.

'Duplication'

This is a disease which started many years ago within the ranks of the lovers of Bugatti cars. Unscrupulous people dismantled a Grand Prix Bugatti into its component parts and with the right hand sold an incomplete car as a 'basket case' and with the left hand sold another incomplete car as 'a box of bits'. The two buyers eventually found suitable second-hand components to replace the missing parts, or had new bits made, and we ended up with two Grand Prix Bugattis where there had only been one. Naturally each owner claims 'authenticity' for his completed car. The Bugatti Owners Club – and the majority of its members – strongly disapprove of this practice.

Unfortunately the disease has spread to many other makes, especially those that were built in large numbers. At best this whole business borders on fraud.

'Destroyed'

A simple enough word that applies to a racing car that has been involved in an accident or fire in which no tangible components are left in recognizable shape or form.

'Scrapped'

This usually applies to a car that is taken out of service by a factory team and either deliberately destroyed so that nothing is left, or useful components are removed and put into store and the rest is thrown on the scrap heap for crushing or melting down. There have been cases of a chassis frame being rescued from the scrap heap and used to re-create a new car. In no way can the new car be described as genuine. If the factory scrapped a car and removed its number from their records, then that car has gone for ever, and a nebulous collection of old and new components can hardly justify the claiming of the scrapped number.

'Broken up'

Similarly, if a factory records that a car has been broken up, it should mean exactly that. It has gone for good.

Maserati 250Fs on the banking at Monza in the 1955 Italian Grand Prix. Nearest the camera is the experimental streamlined car, 2518, driven by Jean Behra.

'Converted'

There have been examples of a Type A model being converted by the factory into a Type B and then into a Type C. The particular car as an entity never disappeared, though it might be difficult to recognize that the Type C was once a Type A. It is virtually impossible to re-convert such a car back to a Type A, no matter how desirable it may be. The perfect example is the E.R.A. that started life as R4B in 1936, was converted to R4C in 1937, and then into R4D in 1938 and was much modified again in 1948. The car still exists as R4D, with a well-documented continuous history, and is as genuine as they come, but it can never revert back to R4B.

A.C.

The Auto Carriers company of Thames Ditton in Surrey were very active with single-seater racing cars in the early 1920s, built in their own toolroom and being very special, with no production parts being used. The engine was a single overhead camshaft 16-valve 4-cylinder, which propelled a very light chassis with a 3-speed gearbox incorporated in the solid rear axle. The final drive was by bevel gears, in direct contrast to the production A.C. cars, which used a worm-drive rear axle. These cars were built specifically for racing on the Brooklands track, particularly in the 200-mile races, and were noted for their slim and slippery bodywork, with long, pointed tails. They were particularly successful in establishing speed records at around 100 mph in the 1500 cc class.

None of the actual Brooklands cars survived, but after the factory withdrew from track racing the racing components were used to build a special car for sprints and hill-climbs. This used a shorter wheelbase and had a two-seater body and was registered for the road, even though it was always in racing trim. Four speeds were incorporated into the rear-axle/gearbox unit, with reverse operated by a separate lever. The methanol-burning 1½-litre engine was as used in the track cars, with the overhead camshaft driven by an inverted-tooth 'silent' chain from the rear of the crankshaft. The bronze head contained four valves per cylinder and twin sparking plugs, the latter fired by twin Delco coil units, and twin Claudel Hobson carburettors were fitted. The block and crankcase were a single aluminium casting, 'wet' steel liners being spigoted in place, and a large aluminium sump was used.

J.A. Joyce at the wheel of the A.C. 16-valve ohc 4-cylinder 1½-litre Sprint car, on the road at Thames Ditton. (The Author's Collection)

Driven by the factory driver J. A. Joyce, this very light sprint car was successful during the mid-1920s, competing all over the UK, from Shelsley Walsh hill-climbs to sprint races on Southport sands.

When it left factory ownership it went to Jack Aked in the north of England, and he converted it into a single-seater. It raced on Southport sands until 1934, when it had a monumental accident due to the original 1921 front axle breaking. A new front axle was made, but otherwise the car remained as it had left the factory. Shortly after this accident the car was put into storage and remained virtually unseen for 40 years, still standing on its original sand-racing knobbly tyres. It is now in a private collection and is occasionally seen on display.

When the A.C. factory were racing these cars and setting records at Brooklands, they made some memorable landmarks, notably 105.14 mph over a flying half-mile in 1921; 94 miles in one hour in 1921; then 101.39 miles in one hour (the first time a 1½-litre car had passed the three-figure mark for one hour's running), and they achieved third place in the 200-mile race in 1923.

In recent years a single-seater A.C. racing car has been built, using standard production components, powered by a side-valve Anzani engine, with an aluminium body styled on the 200-mile race cars. It is a car built on the lines of a factory racing A.C. for the constructor's own pleasure. It was subsequently sold and recently was advertised for sale as a 'Genuine Replica', which is a meaningless description for a home-made A.C. 'Special' which has no identification with the works racing A.C. cars.

All the factory single-seater track racing and record-breaking cars were scrapped. One short-wheelbase sprint car was built and is still in existence.

Sprint Car: 'Genuine'
        1924 Built by the A.C. factory from 1922
                track car components and used by J. A. Joyce
        1930 Acquired by J. Aked.
        1934 Put into storage.
        1974 Acquired by Mrs R. Hewitt.
        1987 Retained by Mrs R. Hewitt.

A.F.M.

When the war finished in 1945 the German motor industry took some time to become rehabilitated and, in Munich, B.M.W.-AG took longer than most to be reorganized. Motor sport was restarted almost immediately by German enthusiasts and one of the pre-war BMW racing engineers, who was still with the firm, set up a private business to enable him to get back in motoring competitions as soon as possible. This was Alex von Falkenhausen, and he formed the firm of A.F.M. standing for *Alex Falkenhausen Motorenbau*. He started off by tuning and modifying pre-war Type 328 B.M.W. sports cars, turning some of them into pure single-seater racing cars, and developing the 6-cylinder engine to run on alcohol fuel.

Eventually he designed and built his own chassis frame and suspension, still using the B.M.W.-based engine. These A.F.M. single-seaters, which were raced by Hans Stuck, the pre-war Auto Union driver, Willy Heeks and others, had a

Hans Stuck with the V-8 AFM in the 1953 International Trophy at Silverstone.
(T. C. March)

multi-tubular frame, independent front suspension by double wishbones and coil springs, and a rear axle of the de Dion layout using torsion bar springs.

As international motor racing got back on to its feet, a Formula 2 was evolved for cars of 2 litre capacity, into which the 328-based-engined cars fitted neatly, but the engine was reaching the end of its useful development life. In co-operation with a designer named Richard Küchen, a 2-litre all-alloy V-8 engine was built, using four overhead camshafts. It was a light and compact unit that fitted neatly into the F2 A.F.M. chassis, similar to those using the B.M.W. 6-cylinder engine. Hans Stuck drove this V-8 car in most of the major Formula 2 races as a factory entry. It proved to be incredibly quick, but rather unreliable in detail items, so that although it usually set the pace, it seldom finished.

The V-8 AFM engine in its later form with two downdraught Weber carburettors.
(The Author)

In the early 1950s Germany and B.M.W. began to get back on to its feet and von Falkenhausen became more and more involved with the reconstitution of the automobile arm of the *Bayerische Motoren Werke* (B.M.W.). He closed down his A.F.M. firm and sold the works single-seater, but before doing so the Küchen V-8 engine was removed, and the car eventually ended up as a Bristol-engined two-seater sports car. The 6-cylinder A.F.M. raced by Willy Heeks, which looked very similar to the V-8 car, was imported into England by John Brown, who passed it on to the Begley brothers. Along the way it lost its special cast-alloy A.F.M. wheels and the nose cowling was altered, while the engine became more and more Bristol and less and less B.M.W. The Begleys raced it in VSCC Historic events in the late fifties, and then it passed to Tony Hutchings, a noted 328 B.M.W. competitor. He had a very high-speed accident in the car and it was severely damaged and for many years lay fallow. In recent years Hutchings has rebuilt it completely, with a new body styled on the original, and sold it back to Germany, to a private collector.
'Genuine'

Acnowledgements to T.T. Workshops, Westbury, Wilts, for information.

A.J.B.

The original A.J.B. was the work of Archie J. Butterworth, an inventor/engineer who lived in Surrey. He was a great four-wheel-drive enthusiast, and to prove his theories just after the war, when few people were interested in 4-W-D, he built a racing car, ostensibly as a sprint and hill-climb machine, though he also used it for circuit racing. His main objective was to prove the advantage of 4-W-D for acceleration purposes.

He took a wartime 4-W-D army Jeep chassis and axles and installed in this an ex-German Army air-cooled Steyr V-8 engine. He improved the Jeep chassis beyond normal recognition, bracing it and stiffening it, and improved the Jeep 4-W-D transmission. The Steyr engine was mounted in the front of the chassis and the Steyr 3-speed gearbox was retained, but behind it he made up a transfer box to step the drive sideways so that it could then run fore and aft to the Jeep axles.

The Steyr engine was of 3.7 litres and the upper half was designed on motor-cycle lines, with separate barrels and cylinder heads, the overhead valves operated by long pushrods from a central camshaft. It was an engine that was asking to be developed and Archie did exactly that. New barrels had the bore increased from 79 mm to 87.5 mm, thus increasing the capacity to 4.5 litres, and a compression ratio of 14 to 1 was used in conjunction with alcohol fuel and a separate Amal motor-cycle carburettor to each cylinder head. A new camshaft was made, giving more exciting valve timing, and nearly 250 bhp was produced. Bodywork was minimal, only the centre of the engine being covered, so that the air-cooled cylinders and heads stuck out in the breeze.

Butterworth used it during the 1948–51 seasons and in spite of the Jeep axles and transmissions being rather heavy for a racing car, he proved his point about acceleration in a most convincing manner. The cornering propensity of 4-W-D was something else and is best described as spectacular, indicating that Archie was fearless and brave. The car made fastest time in the Brighton Speed Trials in 1949

and again in 1951, the latter occasion being in the pouring rain, when the advantages of 4-W-D were indisputable, but it must be remembered that we are talking of the days long before the general public knew what 4-W-D was all about, or any manufacturer had gone into mass production with the system.

Eventually Archie had a very bad crash in the car at the Shelsley Walsh hill-climb in 1951, and that ended the competitive life of the car in England. He sold it to the American Four-Wheel Drive Auto Company in the USA for use by Bill Milliken of the Cornell Aeronautical Laboratory in Buffalo. He used it for experimental purposes and research into 4-W-D, making many alterations and renaming it 'Butterball'. It still exists, on display in an American Museum.

Archie Butterworth went on to make A.J.B. racing engines for other people's specials, much of the knowledge gained with the Steyr engine development going into these flat-four-cylinder air-cooled units.

'Genuine'

Acknowledgements to *Motor Racing Mavericks* by Doug Nye.

Alfa Romeo Tipo P2

The Alfa Romeo firm made a return to Grand Prix racing in 1923 with a new 6-cylinder supercharged car known as the Tipo P1. It was only just ready in time for practice for the Italian Grand Prix and immediately disaster struck, for Ugo Sivocco, racing driver and chief test-driver, crashed and was killed. The entry for the Grand Prix was withdrawn and the car was scrapped.

The brilliant young Vittorio Jano joined the firm, together with Luigi Bazzi, the former being a pure designer and the latter a practical development engineer. Together they made a strong team and in 1924 Alfa Romeo were ready to join in Grand Prix racing once more. This time the new car was a straight-eight cylinder of 2 litres and supercharged to give 140 bhp at 5400 rpm, which was quite exceptional for the time. This was the Tipo P2, and it proved as successful as the Tipo P1 had been unsuccessful, and the team finished 1-2-3-4 in the Italian Grand Prix.

In 1925 the P2 Alfa Romeo team were unbeatable and won the Manufacturers' Championships, after which they withdrew. The Tipo P2 Alfa Romeos were brought out again in 1929–30, when racing was in the doldrums, and were run in various events, more or less in 1925 form.

Only one Tipo P2 has survived and this is kept in working order in the Alfa Romeo museum in Arese. It is often given an airing in historic demonstrations, and the supercharged straight-eight still makes a very healthy and efficient sound.

History

Alfa Romeo Factory Grand Prix team car. Designed and built for the 1924 and 1925 Grand Prix seasons. Reappeared in 1929–30 still as Factory cars. One remaining example owned by the Alfa Romeo firm. On display in museum at Milan-Arese.
'Genuine'

The Alfa Romeo P2, Antonio Ascari at the wheel, at the French Grand Prix at Lyon in 1924. (The Geoffrey Goddard Collection)

Alfa Romeo 'Monza'

In 1931 Vittorio Jano produced a new Alfa Romeo design for sports car racing. This was the 8C-2300, a straight-eight twin-cam engine, with a single super-charger on the right-hand side. It first appeared in the Mille Miglia as a two-seater, but was soon developed into a racing version for Grand Prix events, stripped of its road equipment and carrying only one seat, though the car was still of two-seater width. In Grand Prix guise it appeared for the Italian Grand Prix at Monza and immediately took the unofficial title of 'Monza'. During 1931–32 and 1933 it proved to be very successful and has become so famous and well known that numerous 'Facsimiles' have been built, some from standard 8C-2300 road-going

The Alfa Romeo 'Monza' of Jean-Pierre Wimille at Monte Carlo in 1932. (The Geoffrey Goddard Collection)

sports cars, others from bits and pieces suitably modified to give an air of authenticity. Some are so good that you can only identify them by their chassis numbers. The Alfa Romeo section of the Vintage Sports Car Club keep extensive records from which any 'real' Monza Alfa Romeo can be verified, to weed out the fakes. Other 'Facsimiles' are not very good copies and are easily identified for what they are.

There are still many 'Genuine' Monza Alfa Romeos about, and very reliable and desirable cars they are, either in stripped racing form or as road-equipped two-seaters. However, not every Monza is 'Genuine', even though they may have been built from real Alfa Romeo parts.

The Scuderia Ferrari assembled a series of Monza cars for their own racing team, on behalf of Alfa Romeo, and gave them SF prefixed chassis numbers, which are easily identified. They were raced by the Scuderia until the Tipo B 'Monoposto' came along in 1932 and again in 1933, when the Tipo Bs were withdrawn. Some of the engines were enlarged from 2.3 litres to 2.6 litres.

In round figures, for every four genuine Monza Alfa Romeos there is one fake, which is a good indication of the success of the real ones in the history of motor racing.

'Genuine' cars can be identified by their chassis numbers. Some first-class 'Facsimiles' have been built.

Alfa Romeo Tipo B

The 8C-2300 featured in the previous entry was never intended to be a Grand Prix car, for at the same time Vittorio Jano designed an audacious car for Grand Prix racing, which had two supercharged 6-cylinder 1750 cc sports car engines mounted side by side and geared together. This was the Tipo A, and though it won the 1931 Pescara race it was not a success and was soon abandoned. Jano followed this with the Tipo B, which turned out to be as successful as the Tipo A was unsuccessful, and it became one of the classic Grand Prix cars of all time.

This was a slim single-seater (*monoposto*) with a straight-eight engine somewhat similar to the Monza, but instead of the single supercharger on the right of the engine, the Tipo B had twin superchargers on the left, one for each block of four cylinders. It also had a unique transmission developed from the Tipo A, in which the drive split behind the 4-speed gearbox and two shafts diverged from a gear casing on the back of the box, each shaft running to a crown wheel and pinion unit for each rear wheel, the axle tube joining the two being an empty spacer. The differential was at the transmission dividing point behind the gearbox.

The Tipo B started as a 2.6 litre, and swept the board in 1932, the engine giving 180 bhp at 5400 rpm, and Alfa Romeo then withdrew them, leaving the Scuderia Ferrari, who were running the cars, high and dry. However, before the end of the 1933 season the factory relented and the Tipo B team were back on the scene as successful as ever.

For the new Formula in 1934 the Tipo B was updated, the capacity being increased to 2.9 litres, even though it meant reducing the gearbox to three speeds in order to get strong enough gears within the confines of the existing casing. The bodywork had to be widened to conform with the rules, but even so the *monoposto* was fundamentally the same car, and indeed the 1932 cars were rebuilt to conform to the new specification. Until the German teams of Mercedes-Benz and Auto Union got into their stride midway through the 1934 season, the Tipo B was in complete charge of the scene, and continued to give a good account of itself even into 1935. Development took the form of an engine increase to 3.2 litres, Dubonnet independent front suspension, reversed quarter-elliptic rear suspension and the change from rod-operated brakes to hydraulic operation. The engine of the Tipo B was so flexible that in overall operation the 3-speed gearbox proved adequate, though it could be a handicap on short twisty circuits.

Seen in the paddock at Brooklands in 1935 is Dick Shuttleworth's Alfa Romeo Tipo B, chassis 50007. Note the Brooklands silencer and fishtail. (The Geoffrey Goddard Collection)

After the works-supported Scuderia Ferrari abandoned the Tipo B in 1936 in favour of the newer 8C/35, the old cars were sold off and raced in amateur hands right through to the end of the 1939 season, and naturally carried on into Historic Racing. Most of the *monoposto* Tipo B cars have led well-documented lives, even though they were dispersed as far afield as Australia, North America, South America and Great Britain. One superb 'Facsimile' has been built in recent years that is so good that it almost passes as an original car, especially when viewed alongside some of the real *monoposto* Tipo B cars that have been modified and 'improved' over the years. Indeed many people, who don't worry about origins and details, accept this 'Facsimile' as being the real thing, which it clearly is not.

History

According to the Alfa Romeo factory records, six cars were built in 1932, with enough spare parts for three major rebuilds. In 1934 seven cars were built, with a spares pool capable of rebuilding four cars, but it seems that two more cars were completed. In 1935 one of the 1932 cars and three of the 1934 cars were rebuilt with I.F.S. and the remaining five 1934 cars were rebuilt to various later specifications. Eight cars are known to still exist, in full working order; one was converted into a Special in 1937–39 and still exists; three exist in semi-derelict condition or are being 'reclaimed'; two (possibly three) are known to have been destroyed and there is one 'Facsimile'.

1932 cars	Chassis 5001	Went to South America early in its life. Uprated in 1935. Came to UK in recent years with some parts missing. Restored and new parts made. 'Authentic'.
	Chassis 5002	Uprated in 1935 with I.F.S. Went to Australia. In late sixties came to UK less engine. Completed with the rear engine from the *Bi-motore* Alfa Romeo. 'Authentic'.
	Chassis 5003	From Ferrari to Raymond Sommer; Chris Staniland in 1936; Rebuilt into Multi-Union I in 1938 and rebuilt again into Multi-Union II in 1939. Still in this form.
	Chassis 5004	Untraced. Probably broken up.
	Chassis 5005	Still in 1932 narrow-body form and retained by Alfa Romeo SpA. 'Genuine'.
	Chassis 5006	Raced by Georges 'Raph' in France after leaving Ferrari. To UK in 1939. Very active in historic racing until it went to Japan to join a private collection. 'Genuine'.
1934 cars:	Chassis 50001	In UK after Ferrari but not raced, engine used in a racing motor-boat. Less engine to USA in 1955. Still in private collection in USA. 'Authentic'.
	Chassis 50002	Raced by Villapadierna of Spain in 1936. Went to USA in 1939 and competed at Indianapolis. Also ran there in later years. Eventually became semi-derelict, losing its engine and its distinctive Tipo B rear axle. 'Unrestored'.

The straight-eight engine of the Tipo B made with two blocks of four cylinders and with twin superchargers. (The Author)

Chassis 50003   From Ferrari to Charlie Martin in 1936. Raced by him in UK and other events. Bought by Jack Bartlett and raced in 1939. Went to Australia after the war. Raced and rebuilt. Returned to UK and still in continual use in Historic racing. 'Genuine'.

Chassis 50004   Went to USA from Ferrari in 1937. Stayed there and raced often. Time saw the engine and gearbox disappear. In private collection with sports Alfa Romeo engine and gearbox installed. 'Authentic'.

Chassis 50005   Uprated in 1935 with I.F.S. From Ferrari to UK to Austin Dobson in 1936. Raced by Kenneth Evans 1937 to 1939. Post-war raced by Roy Salvadori. Then to New Zealand, where it is today in superb condition. 'Genuine'.

Chassis 50006   Uprated in 1935 with I.F.S. From Ferrari to UK. Raced and modified by Frank Ashby until 1939. Post-war used in hill-climbs by Ken Hutchison and club racing by John Goodhew. Then to Australia. Still there in museum collection. 'Genuine'.

Chassis 50007   From Ferrari to UK. Raced by Dick Shuttleworth in 1935 and 1936. Post-war converted into a two-seater road-going sports car without destroying its originality. Went to USA. In 1980 converted back to '*monoposto*'. Active in UK Historic racing. 'Genuine'.

Chassis 50008   Untraced.

Chassis 50009   Uprated in 1935 with I.F.S. From Ferrari to Argentina in 1936. Virtually destroyed by fire in a crash in 1951. Various bits remain.

Chassis 50009R   'Facsimile' built by Rodney Felton from used spare parts and newly manufactured parts.

Alfa Romeo Bi-motore

When the Alfa Romeo factory began to lose their supremacy in Grand Prix racing to the German Mercedes-Benz and Auto Union teams in 1935, the Scuderia Ferrari, who were running the factory Alfa Romeos, decided to build two special cars that would match the German cars, even though they would not be eligible for the Formula Grand Prix events, due to their being over 750 kilograms in weight. The project was in the nature of the face-saver for Alfa Romeo and Ferrari, and the Italian nation. There were two important events on the international calendar at the time that were not run to the Formula rules, these being the *Avusrennen*, run on the outskirts of Berlin, and the Tripoli Grand Prix in North Africa. The German teams were using their Grand Prix cars in both these events, together with some non-Formula experimental cars, but Ferrari went for out-and-out non-Formula specials, designed by Luigi Bazzi at the Modena factory utilizing Alfa Romeo racing components. It was hoped that these 'specials' would humiliate the German teams in their own capital city, and show the Libyans in North Africa that Italy really was a master race.

In a lengthened Tipo B chassis frame two Grand Prix engines were installed, one in the normal position in the front and the other turned about face and mounted in the rear, with the driving seat between them; hence the simple but explicit name *Bi-motore*, pronounced 'Bee-mo-tory'. A single gearbox was attached to the rear of the front engine and the rear engine drove forwards into this gearbox. Two output shafts came from the gearbox, angled left and right, to run to the independently sprung rear wheels. A dog-clutch was used to disconnect the engines for starting purposes. Fuel for this monster was carried in two long tanks, one on each side of the chassis between the front and rear wheels. The engines in the first car were normal 2.9-litre straight-eight supercharged Grand Prix Alfa Romeo units, as used in the Tipo B cars. A second car was built using two 3.2-litre versions of the same engine design. Front suspension of the *Bi-motore* was by the Dubonnet independent system using a tubular cross-beam with coil-spring units enclosed in oil-filled containers, which supplied the damping. Rear suspension was by semi-elliptic leaf springs, each wheel being carried on its own hub unit.

Not surprisingly the *Bi-motore* proved to be immensely fast, but it devoured its rear tyres at a phenomenal rate and any speed advantage it had over the German cars was lost in repeated stops for new tyres. As a non-Formula 'prestige car' it was a bit of a white elephant and the two cars only appeared during the 1935 season, the 'big' one driven by Tazio Nuvolari and the 'small' one by Louis Chiron. Some 'face-saving' was achieved by Nuvolari when he took some short-distance records at 200 mph, especially as they had been held by the Germans previously. In racing the best they could achieve was fourth at Tripoli (Nuvolari) and second at Avus (Chiron).

In 1937 one of these cars was purchased by the English driver Austin Dobson and he attempted to use it in British races, actually taking part in road-circuit events with it, as well as running it in events on the Brooklands banked track. The car he bought was fitted with 2.9-litre engines and had had the front suspension changed for the 1936 Grand Prix pattern of trailing arms and coil springs. The remains of the second car were scrapped.

It was not a success, even in British handicap events, and in 1938 Dobson sold the car to the Hon. Peter Aitken, who had Thomson & Taylor of Brooklands Track rebuild, or more accurately, reconstruct it into a *Mono-motore* by cutting it in half and creating what became known as the Alfa-Aitken. In this form it was

Austin Dobson's Alfa Romeo Bi-motore *seen shortly after its arrival in England in 1937.* (The Geoffrey Goddard Collection)

quite successful after the war, and then it went to New Zealand, where it languished for many years, having been fitted with a G.M.C. truck engine after the Alfa Romeo engine blew up. In the 1970s the remains were acquired by Tom Wheatcroft as representing the *Bi-motore*, but in truth what he got were the bones of the Alfa-Aitken. The front suspension was there, and the shortened chassis frame, but little else, but undaunted he set about 're-creating' the *Bi-motore* with the aid of the Alfa Romeo museum and numerous Alfa Romeo enthusiasts and specialists. Two new engines were made, a new rear part of the chassis was built, and entirely new gearbox/transfer gear assembly, new rear axle and rear suspension, new fuel tanks, new radiators and new bodywork. This is a true 'Reconstruction' in the best possible manner and a monument to the enthusiasm and tenacity of the builders, even though it can never be considered a true or genuine *Bi-motore*.

While this 'Reconstruction' was in progress the Alfa Romeo factory museum in Italy was also constructing a *Bi-motore*, though their's was from scratch, with no original bits, and was purely for display purposes. Thus we now have two *Bi-motore* Alfa Romeos in existence, though neither of them are 'Genuine' cars. However, for the student of motor racing history, they are honourable efforts, for without them it is doubtful whether anyone would really believe such cars existed, in spite of the many fine contemporary photographs.

History

Two cars built by the Scuderia Ferrari in Modena, using Alfa Romeo components, in 1935. One car sold to the UK in 1937, the other scrapped. The UK car rebuilt into the single-engined Alfa-Aitken in 1939. Very active after the war and then went to New Zealand. The bones returned to UK and resurrected.

Bi-motore No. 1.   Built by Scuderia Ferrari with two 2.9-litre engines. Second at Avus 1935 driven by Chiron.

Bi-motore No. 2.   Built by Scuderia Ferrari with two 3.2-litre engines. Fourth at Tripoli GP 1935 driven by Nuvolari. Used for record breaking.

Bi-motore No. 3   A 'Facsimile' of a *Bi-motore* built by the Alfa Romeo factory for their museum at Arese. Not a 'replica built by the original artist', as the original cars were built at the Scuderia Ferrari in Modena.

NB. Either No. 1 or No. 2, or an amalgam of both, came to England in 1937 and eventually became the Alfa-Aitken.

Alfa Romeo Tipo 8C/35

By 1935 the Tipo B was outclassed in Grand Prix racing under normal conditions and Vittorio Jano produced a logical successor. It still had a straight-eight-cylinder engine with twin superchargers, but it was of 3.8 litres capacity and was mounted in an entirely new chassis, with trailing link independent front suspension and swing-axle independent rear suspension, with traverse leaf-spring at the rear and oil-immersed coil springs at the front. The chassis frame was tubular on what became known as the 'ladder-frame' principle and the bodywork was designed to cover all the mechanical components, including the suspensions. This was the 8C/35 and a team of these new models eventually supplanted the successful Tipo B cars.

Only one of the 8C/35 cars seems to have survived intact (ch. no. 50013), and when it was sold to the Swiss amateur racing driver Hans Ruesch it was said to be the works car that had won the 1936 Coppa Ciano race. Ruesch won the 1936 Donington Park Grand Prix with this car, partnered by Dick Seaman, and the following year raced in many British events, lending it to other drivers when he could not make the journey from Switzerland. In 1939 it was sold to Robert Arbuthnot, but the war cut short his activity with it.

After the war Dennis Poore acquired this car and spent a lot of money on developing the engine, with different superchargers and manifolding. He used it in airfield racing and in the RAC Hill-climb Championship, which he won in 1950, using a pre-selector gearbox mounted between the engine and the Alfa Romeo gearbox, which was in unit with the chassis-mounted differential unit.

Following a remarkably successful period as a hill-climb car, this 8C/35 was used in Historic Racing events until Dennis Poore retired it from racing in 1955, since when it has never run again in public, although it is still owned by him.

In 1936 Alfa Romeo produced a brand new 4-litre V-12 engine which fitted in the 8C/35 chassis. It was a good car, but too late, for the German technical advance was outstripping everyone. The Scuderia Ferrari raced the 12C/36 until the end of the 750 kilogram Formula, but did not achieve a great measure of success. Although some bits of a 12-cylinder car have been found, no complete car has survived. The 8C/35 is recognized by its high-level outside exhaust pipe on the right-hand side, while the 12C had pipes on each side running low under the sides of the body, otherwise the cars looked identical.

Dick Seaman at the wheel of Hans Ruesch's ex-Scuderia Ferrari Alfa Romeo 8C/35 in the 1936 Donington Grand Prix. (The Geoffrey Goddard Collection)

In 1987 the remains of an 8C/35 Alfa Romeo were retrieved from South America by an English enthusiast, and though not a complete car there are enough original bits to re-create an authentic car.

Alfa Romeo Tipo 158 and 159

By the time of the new Grand Prix Formula in 1938, the Alfa Romeo firm and Scuderia Ferrari were parting company and Ferrari decided to concentrate on 1500 cc 'voiturette' racing rather than continue banging his head against the wall trying to keep up with Mercedes-Benz and Auto Union. The young engineer Giaocchino Colombo was seconded to the Scuderia Ferrari in Modena and a 'voiturette' was designed and built that turned out to be a little jewel. Alfa Romeo, under the Spanish engineer Wilfredo Ricart, was pressing on in Grand Prix racing with a 3-litre V-16 engine, amongst others, and the new 1500 cc 'voiturette' was virtually one half of the Grand Prix engine, the beautiful little straight-eight having a single supercharger on the left of the cylinder block. The tubular chassis was mini-Grand Prix design, with trailing link I.F.S. and swing-axle rear suspension, using transverse leaf springs at both ends, and the prettiest of single-seater bodies clothed it.

Juan Fangio (Alfa Romeo 158) in the wet at the 1950 International Trophy at Silverstone. He finished second to team-mate Farina. (T. C. March)

Another view of Juan Fangio, this time at the wheel of the Tipo 159 that he drove into second place in the 1951 British Grand Prix at Silverstone. (T. C. March)

Known officially as the Tipo 158 it was soon christened 'Alfetta' when it appeared late in the 1938 season at the Coppa Ciano at Livorno. After a few initial teething troubles it dominated 'voiturette' racing, continuing into 1940, when Italy was still out of the European war. When racing resumed in 1946 the Tipo 158 Alfa Romeo team was soon re-formed, run by Alfa Romeo themselves, and after an initial failure the team recovered to win every race they entered until the middle of 1951. So successful was the Tipo 158 team that Alfa Romeo withdrew for 1949 and returned in 1950, to continue to win every race in which they competed. By 1951 the little 1½-litre engine had been stretched to its limit, and the new 4½-litre Ferrari cars, running without the advantage of high-pressure supercharging, became a serious threat to the all-conquering Tipo 158. Development on two-stage supercharging, de Dion rear suspension, fatter and more bulbous bodywork to contain enormous fuel tankage had caused the cars to be completely changed in character from the diminutive little model that first appeared in 1938, but horsepower had gone up from 170 bhp to 380 bhp, with fleeting glimpses of over 400 bhp on the test-bed. In the middle of 1951 they were finally defeated by Ferrari, but they fought back to the end of the season and went out bloody but unbowed. The withdrawal of the Alfa Romeo team at the end of 1951 saw the premature death knell to Formula One of the supercharged/unsupercharged equivalency Formula.

Alfa Romeo never sold a Tipo 158 or 159, though many people tried hard to buy one, and when they withdrew from Grand Prix racing engine development continued as the engines from the cars were used in racing and record-breaking speedboats. Fortunately the firm kept one car in full working order, and others in their fine museum at Arese. At least once a year the 159 is brought out to give a demonstration, and it is something that no Historic racing enthusiast should miss. The sound alone of that two-stage supercharged, alcohol burning, straight-eight engine is still something that gets the adrenalin flowing.

For 18 months an Alfa Romeo enthusiast with factory connections since 1951, negotiated to acquire a Tipo 158 that had been lying fallow at the Portello factory in Milan. Early in 1987 it arrived safely in London, thus refuting the positive statement made at the beginning of the previous paragraph.

'Genuine'

Alfa-Aitken

When the Hon. Peter Aitken acquired the *Bi-motore* Alfa Romeo from Austin Dobson it was not with the intention of racing it. The previous owner had illustrated pretty conclusively that the twin-engined monster was not suited to British racing. Aitken gave the car to Thomson & Taylor, the Brooklands engineering firm, and they used it to build what was in effect a *Mono-motore*. The car was virtually cut in half, the entire rear end and rear engine being discarded, as well as the complicated gearbox/transfer box unit. An E.N.V. pre-selector gearbox was mounted behind the forward engine and this drove to a conventional rear axle mounted on quarter-elliptic leaf springs extending rearwards from the abbreviated chassis frame. The car was clothed in a rather bulbous bodywork, with a rather fat and puffed-up radiator cowl, and it bore no resemblance at all to the *Bi-motore* from which it had been born, even though the engine, chassis and front suspension were all unchanged.

It was finished in midsummer 1939 and Peter Aitken drove at the last meeting to be held at the Brooklands track, in August 1939. War then intervened and the car was put into store. Aitken died during the war years, and when racing resumed the car appeared at Britain's first race meeting, on Gransden Lodge airfield, and R. V. Wallington won a race with it. In 1947 Tony Rolt acquired the car and had Freddie Dixon enlarge the engine from 2.9 litres to 3.4 litres and convert it from supercharging to eight SU carburettors, thus making the car eligible for the new Formula One. Rolt raced it in this form quite successfully and when it became out-classed and obsolete it was sold to New Zealand, where it was virtually raced into the ground, ending up with a GMC truck engine replacing the straight-eight Alfa Romeo engine. It finally deteriorated and languished in a semi-derelict state until it was acquired by Tom Wheatcroft in the 1970s. It was bought as representing the remains of the *Bi-motore*, but in truth it was merely the bones of the Alfa-Aitken, and not even complete at that. There were no engines, no gearbox or transfer gears, no rear axle assembly, suspension or rear of the chassis, and no bodywork or fuel tanks.

With the aid of numerous Alfa Romeo enthusiasts, Tom Wheatcroft caused a *Bi-motore* to be created from the ashes. The Alfa-Aitken has gone forever. 'Scrapped'

Allard

Sydney Allard's principal activity with his Allard Motor Company was the build-ing of touring, saloon and sports cars on a production basis, but from an early age his real interest lay in competition motoring. It was no surprise when he carried on an active competition season while he was setting up his production car business after the Second World War. The chance to acquire two interesting engines from the German army started his thoughts on a pure sprint and hill-climb single-seater, as distinct from his previous specials, which were modified versions of his production cars.

These engines were air-cooled V-8 units made by the Austrian Steyr firm and used in military vehicles, but Sydney Allard could see that they were capable of withstanding a lot of development work. The pushrod-operated overhead valves were in hemispherical combustion chambers in individual alloy cylinder heads, so

Sydney Allard with the V-8 Steyr-Allard at Shelsley Walsh in June 1947. With this car Allard won the RAC Hill Climb Championship in 1949. (Guy Griffiths)

that in effect the Steyr engine was like eight motorcycle units on a one-piece crank-case. It was 1946 and the following winter saw a single-seater chassis constructed from Ford components, which were being used in the Allard sports cars. One of the tuned Steyr engines was installed in this new Allard special and it appeared at a test-day at Prescott Hill-climb on 25 April, 1947.

Called the Steyr-Allard, its first competition was at Prescott on 11 May, 1947, and it set up a new record for the hill. In 1948 it was further developed with a de Dion rear axle layout in place of the orthodox Ford beam axle, and it continued to be a regular competitor in the British Hill Climb Championship. Two more Steyr engines were acquired to provide spares for the racing unit and to keep pace with the increased power output. In 1949 Sydney more than justified all the work and expense that had gone into the Steyr-Allard when he won the RAC Hill Climb Championship, scoring 39 points to the 33 of the runner-up.

By 1950 Sydney had become involved with sports car racing, so his hill-climbing activities had to take second place. He was unable to take part in all the Championship rounds, but still finished second. The car had now served him well for four seasons, and during this time a new hill-climb special had been started, but progress was slow due to other work taking priority. For the 1951 season the Steyr-Allard was drastically modified using parts and ideas from the stillborn special. This involved four-wheel drive, using a Willys-Jeep front axle with free-wheel units derived from Rover parts in the hubs. The axle was sprung on coil springs and an electromagnetic clutch arrangement and transfer box took the drive fore and aft, the rear end being unchanged. All this mechanism added 200 lb to the weight of the car, and the end result was a rather complicated car that was not much quicker up the hills than the original.

This unsuccessful season was really the end of the Steyr-Allard as a works car, and in 1953 it was sold to Dr. Pinkerton, who continued to run it in 4-W-D form, but the following year he passed it on to Doug Wilcox, who put it back to rear drive only, removing the Jeep front end and replacing the split-Ford ifs beam layout. The car was now nine years old and was no longer competitive, and it more or less

disappeared. Ten years later, in 1964, Sydney Allard bought the car back and let one of his design staff, Dave Hooper, use it on the Drag Racing scene. After that it was Sydney's idea that it should go to the National Motor Museum at Beaulieu, but before this happened he was taken ill and died in the spring of 1966. With his death the Allard Motor Company collapsed and in the ensuing months of sorting things out the Steyr-Allard was forgotten. It never did get to the museum, but 'went to ground', having been removed from Dave Hooper's home. It resurfaced in 1984.
'Genuine'

Acknowledgement to: *Allard – The Inside Story* by Tom Lush, Motor Racing Publications.

Alta

Like many small manufacturers of racing cars, Geoffrey Taylor started by building himself a special in the form of a competition two-seater sports car. He was particularly ambitious as a special-builder in that he made his own engine as well as the rest of the car. It was an 1100 cc four-cylinder with twin overhead camshafts, and was subsequently supercharged and enlarged to 1500 cc. This began in 1931 and it wasn't long before he built a second car for a customer; then the Alta Car & Engineering Company at Tolworth was under way.

By 1935 he had developed his sports car into a 1500 cc and had changed the drive to the camshafts from gears to a roller-chain and the whole engine was built from light alloy, so it was a comparatively simple step to his first single-seater. By moving the engine slightly to the left and making a special rear axle with offset differential housing, he was able to sit the driver down between the propeller shaft and the chassis side rail, and with front and rear axles being mounted above the chassis frame on their leaf springs, so the resultant car was very low and the width was kept to a minimum.

Six of these 'offset' cars were built, and his next step was a pure single-seater with the driver sitting centrally over the propshaft. This Alta model had independent suspension to all four wheels by means of coil springs on vertical sliders, supported by two large cross-tubes. Three of these models were built, the third having the channel-section frame replaced by a tubular frame. When war broke out in 1939 another new model was nearly finished, this having independent suspension to all four wheels by means of box-section members swinging on large cross-tubes, operating torsion bar springs. This car was completed during the war and appeared on the immediate post-war racing scene.

Once again Taylor's ingenuity and design ability came to the fore with an entirely new car for the post-war racing scene. On a tubular chassis frame developed from the 1939 car, wishbone suspension was used for all four wheels, the unusual feature being the use of rubber blocks in compression as the springing medium. Since making his first single-seater, all Geoffrey Taylor's cars had been supercharged, whether 1500 cc or 2000 cc, and for the post-war cars a system of two-stage supercharging was devised. With Formula 2 becoming strong in 1952 Taylor was quick to offer for sale his rubber-sprung car with an unsupercharged 2-litre, 4-cylinder engine, complying with the Formula 2 rules.

The 1936 Alta 1½-litre driven by Johnny Wakefield on the Brooklands Campbell Circuit in 1937. (The Author's Collection)

Geoffrey Taylor in the paddock at Brooklands with the 1937 all-independently sprung, single-seater 1.5-litre Alta. (The Geoffrey Goddard Collection)

A continual lack of capital meant that every Alta was built to order and limitations of staff meant that delivery was rather slow, so that production was very limited. After making three supercharged 1500 cc cars for Formula 1, two of them with two-stage supercharging, five Formula 2 cars were built, bringing the total production of racing single-seater Altas to 18.

The Alta engine used an aluminium crankcase-cum-block, into which steel wet-liners were fixed, so that engine capacity was a simple matter of which diameter liners were used, in conjunction with which particular crankshaft. The original sports engines had gear drive to the overhead camshafts, but by the time the single-seaters appeared this drive was changed to a single-row roller chain. It was a light engine and gave good power, but lack of money prevented the best materials being used and reliability was not one of its greatest assets. The Alta car was very successful in short-circuit races at places like the Crystal Palace and the Campbell

Bob Cowell with the ex-Lady Mary Grosvenor 2-litre Alta at Shelsley Walsh in September, 1946. (Guy Griffiths)

and Mountain circuits at Brooklands, but it had a poor record in long races. In sprints and hill-climbs the Altas were strong contenders for Fastest Time of the Day. In unsupercharged Formula 2 form for post-war racing they had enough power, but the rest of the car was too heavy; none the less they gave many drivers the opportunity to gain experience with proper single-seater racing cars as distinct from home-made specials. In addition to building racing cars Taylor offered the engine for sale to other manufacturers and H.W.M. and Connaught used Alta engines with fair success.

With each car being hand-built to customer requirements no two cars were identical and with only 18 cars being built as pure single-seater racing cars, each one had its own identity from the day the chassis was laid down until today, or whenever it disappeared from the racing scene. With the engine being the most fragile part of the car, especially the post-war ones, some of them were turned into specials, or parts were used to construct specials, so that some of the cars have virtually disappeared.

History

Manufactured by the Alta Car & Engineering Company of Tolworth, Surrey. Six 'offset' cars built, of which one was developed into a sprint/hill-climb special and three remain in original form. Four pre-war central-seat cars were built, three with coil-spring suspension and one with torsion bar suspension, each one distinctive and well known. Three have survived and one was broken up and used as the basis for a road car. Of the three post-war Formula 1 cars none remained, though parts of one are in a resurrected car. Of the post-war Formula 2 cars only two remain intact.

Chassis No. 52S	'Genuine.' An 'offset' car built for A. J. Cormack. Now in Australia.
No. 53S	'Genuine.' An 'offset' car built for R. R. Jackson – very active post-war in VSCC events and hill-climbs. Now in Swiss museum.

No. 56S	'Genuine.' An 'offset' car built for J. P. Wakefield. Took Shelsley Walsh Ladies' Record in 1939. Fitted with post-war engine by the factory. Now in Australia.
No. 57S	Whereabouts unknown. An 'offset' car built for J. H. Bartlett (2 litre).
No. 58S	'Authentic.' An 'offset' car built for F. O'Boyle. Fitted with Alta I.F.S. in 1938. Used by Taylor with first post-war 2-litre engine. Became the basis for the Norris Special built by John Norris.
No. 59S	'Scrapped.' An 'offset' car built for P. Jucker (2 litre). Used by Taylor as works development car up to 1939.
No. 61IS	'Genuine.' Single-seater with all-independent suspension by coil springs – built for P. Jucker, 1937. Crashed in I.o.M. in 1937 and driver killed. Rebuilt for George Abecassis in 1938. Most famous of all Altas. Raced until 1939 and again in 1946 by Abecassis. Still in existence in 1946 form and owned by VSCC member.
No. 62IS	'Genuine.' Single-seater with all-independent suspension by coil springs – built for Hugh Hunter and fitted with special body by R. R. Jackson and Zillwood Milledge, in 1938. Rebodied post-war and quite active in Historic Racing. Owned by VSCC member.
No. 67IS	'Resurrection.' Single-seater with tubular chassis frame and all-independent suspension by coil springs. Built for Tony Beadle (2 litre). Potentially the best Alta of them all. Raced by Beadle until 1939. Post-war raced by Noel Carr and others. Broken up by Paul Emery and used as the basis for an Aston Martin-engined road car. Being resurrected by a VSCC member.
No. 69IS	Whereabouts unknown. 'Single-seater with independent suspension all-round by torsion bar springs. Built for Lady Mary Grosvenor (2 litre), but not delivered and

John Heath with the 1948 Alta 1½-litre Grand Prix car in that year's British Empire Trophy in the Isle of Man. (The Geoffrey Goddard Collection)

The Formula 2 Alta of Tony Gaze in the paddock at Goodwood in 1951. (Guy Griffiths)

was last Alta to be built pre-war. Post-war raced by Bob Cowell and Gordon Watson. Rebodied with post-war Alta-style bodywork and disappeared into limbo at end of supercharged era of racing.

No. GP1   'Resurrection.' First post-war car built for George Abecassis as supercharged 1500 cc Formula 1 car 1948. At end of Formula used as basis for Jaguar-powered sports car and became modified out of all recognition. Front half used to re-create GP 1 for the Donington Museum.

No. GP 2   'Scrapped.' Built for Geoffrey Crossley, who raced it in Formula 1 until 1951. Subsequently broken up and parts used in a special.

No. GP 3   'Scrapped.' Built for Joe Kelly with two-stage supercharger layout. Subsequently broken up and parts used in a special.

No. GP 4   Not completed. Became F2/3 Formula 2 car.

No. F2/1   Unsupercharged 2-litre 1952 Formula 2 car built for Tony Gaze. Engine put in H.W.M. and rest of car used to make Jaguar-engined sports car.

No. F2/2   Unsupercharged 2-litre 1952 Formula 2 car built for Gordon Watson. Used in Historic racing, still in private hands.

No. F2/3   Started life as GP 4. Built as unsupercharged 2-litre 1952 Formula 2 car for A. J. Stokes.

No. F2/4   Unsupercharged 2-litre 1952 Formula 2 car built for Oliver Simpson.

No. F2/5   'Authentic.' Unsupercharged 2-litre 1952 Formula 2 car. Last car built by Geoffrey Taylor for Peter Whitehead. Unique in having alloy wheels. Engine put into F2 Cooper and rest of car sold to Australia. Ended up with Holden engine installed. Returned to UK and resurrected with H.W.M.-Alta engine, 2 litre with gear-driven camshafts.

Alvis

The Alvis company was very active in competitions in the 1920s and their early developments were based on the 12/50 model, which was to become their best-known sports model. The production 12/50 had a bore and stroke of 69 × 110 mm, but the racing versions were reduced to 1½ litres by using a bore and stroke of 68 × 103 mm. The works Alvis entry won the 1923 JCC 200-mile race at Brooklands at a speed of 93.29 mph. The factory continued to race the 12/50-based car in 1924, but then branched out into complicated and advanced front-wheel-drive cars. A production F.W.D. model was marketed alongside the more orthodox 12/50.

One of the special works 12/50-engined racing cars, built for the 1924 JCC 200-mile race, was later used at Brooklands by the Dunlop Rubber Company as a high-speed test-car for evaluating tyres. After lying fallow for many years this car was resurrected in recent times, and restored to better than new condition. Not only is it capable of winning races in today's VSCC events, but it is a worthy contender in any Concours competition.

A pre-race factory publicity shot of one of the 1923 Alvis 200-mile race cars. (The Geoffrey Goddard Collection)

Another historic Alvis that is still in competition today is a 1923 ex-works car, rebuilt into the configuration of the start of the Alvis factory racing efforts, without front-wheel brakes, a 'bolster' fuel tank and much-drilled chassis frame. Both these cars originate from original cars, but have been 'restored' with new parts, and a new body in the case of the 1924 car.

Amilcar Six

The little sports Amilcars, with their lusty little side-valve engines, were very popular in the early 1920s, and the marque had a strong following. To project the sporting image of the name the firm took part in all manner of competitions with factory cars, and tackled serious racing events with a little jewel of a car. This was the Amilcar Six.

The six-cylinder engine had twin overhead camshafts and a supercharger mounted on the front of the crankcase. It was a pure racing engine, of 1100 cc capacity for the popular 'voiturette' category of the twenties and was mounted in a special low chassis that was a scaled-down Grand Prix car of the time, with the driver sitting low down alongside the propshaft. The factory raced a special offset version, as well as production-based cars, for the Amilcar Six was offered for sale in stripped racing form and road-equipped for sports car racing. They were beautifully made little cars, splendidly proportioned, and built almost regardless of cost. It was almost guaranteed that a blown Amilcar Six would win the 1100 cc class in any event that it entered.

A few of them found their way to England, and a couple of them were very active at Brooklands and elsewhere right up to 1939. In the immediate post-war period of British club events the car illustrated, with road equipment, was a regular competitor driven by Owen Finch. While the sight of an Amilcar Six is rare these days, they do occasionally appear in VSCC events and these miniature vintage Grand Prix cars are well worth a close study. The sound from the engine and exhaust is nice as well.

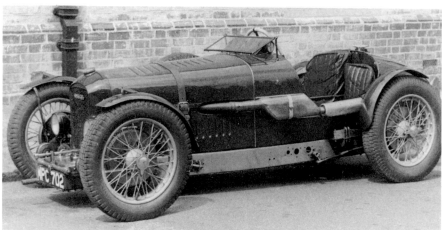

An Amilcar 6-cylinder supercharged twin-cam car seen here in road-going trim. (Guy Griffiths)

Normally, if you see an Amilcar Six it is pretty genuine, but recently the 'Facsimile trade' has turned its attention to these lovely little cars and one has appeared that has been built up from an assortment of parts and another spurious one has appeared with a 4-cylinder engine in it!

Appleton Special

In 1934 John Appleton acquired an 1100 cc sports/racing two-seater Maserati which, while it was a nicely made little car, was dreadfully underpowered for its size and weight. The pretty little supercharged straight-eight twin-overhead camshaft engine was very reluctant to give much power, so Appleton removed it and substituted a racing Riley 9 engine, at the same time replacing the Maserati gearbox with an E.N.V. pre-selector gearbox, as used on the sports Rileys of the time. A Zoller supercharger was installed, to blow some 25 psi into the Riley engine. The Maserati chassis was of two-seater width, with the driver sitting alongside the propshaft, and for 1935 Appleton continued to use the car in this chassis form, calling the car a Riley-Maserati 1100 cc.

Results were promising and the following year the car underwent an enormous rebuild, emerging showing very little of its ancestry. The chassis frame was narrowed to a slim single-seater, the back springs being mounted on outriggers and the Maserati axles and springs being retained front and rear. A single-seater body was built, and Robin Jackson of Brooklands fame continued the development of the engine. By now there was very little visible of the Maserati ancestry, the chassis rails being lightened extensively by means of drilling holes everywhere, so the car became the Appleton Special.

The entry of R. J. W. Appleton and his Appleton Special became a regular feature of British national racing from 1935 to 1939, and in addition John Appleton took some International 1100 cc class records for the standing-start kilometre and mile. While the car was by no means a lightweight, its acceleration was remarkable, indicating that Jackson was getting a lot of power from the supercharged Riley engine.

As development continued the weak points of the Riley unit began to show, and parts were redesigned to withstand the power output. The biggest step was the designing and making of a special crankshaft with a centre main-bearing to fit in a modified Riley crankcase, that normally had no provision for a centre bearing on the Riley crankshaft. New connecting rods and piston were made at the same time, to go with the more robust crankshaft, and in 1938 the car was rebodied with a slimmer and smoother single-seater body with fashionable head-fairing on the shapely tail. With a blower giving 27 psi and alcohol fuel the power output was up to 160 bhp, which was way ahead of most contemporary 1100 cc engines. The short-pushrod valve gear of the original Riley design was retained, operated by the two camshafts mounted high up in the cylinder block. An inter-cooler was used between the blower and the engine, and this protruded out into the airstream on the right-hand side of the bonnet.

By the end of the 1939 season the Appleton Special was in a very high state of tune, almost too high in fact, and its reliability came into question. On the test-bed Jackson had seen a brief reading of 183 bhp from the 1100 cc 4-cylinder, but it was becoming problematical keeping it all inside the iron-block engine.

John Appleton's Riley-powered Appleton Special in its 1938 form. (The Geoffrey Goddard Collection)

After the war John Appleton sold the car, and it never performed the same again, as it lacked the expertise and facilities of Robin Jackson's establishment. After many years of just 'being about the place', the blown 1100 cc engine was taken out by one of the owners, and it disappeared. The car changed hands a number of times and eventually an owner installed a fairly normal sports Riley 1½-litre engine, the rest of the car being unchanged from its 1939 form. When a supercharger was added to the 1½-litre Riley engine the car began to show some of its old form, though in a larger category than it had been used to.

It is still owned by a VSCC member, still has the 1½-litre blown Riley engine installed, and is occasionally seen in historic events.

This was one of the better specials ever built, and certainly one of the most successful in its heyday.

Aston-Butterworth

The name of these specials was simple in the extreme; Bill Aston made the chassis and Archie Butterworth made the engines. Bill Aston had been racing 500 cc and 1100 cc J.A.P.-engined Coopers, but had ideas of going into the current Formula 2 of 1952, which allowed a capacity of 2 litres without supercharging. The chassis frame was basically Cooper-Bristol Formula 2, with Cooper suspension front and rear by transverse leaf spring and lower wishbones. The engine was an air-cooled flat-four with pushrod-operated overhead valves, designed and built by Archie Butterworth, who had made quite a name for himself with his air-cooled Steyr V-8 A.J.B. four-wheel-drive sprint car. The engine was mounted in the front of the chassis and was coupled to an M.G. TC gearbox, with open shaft running under the central seat to the Cooper chassis-mounted differential unit. With a fuel tank in the tail, a simple and neat aluminium body was made and the Aston-Butterworth was created.

Bill Aston had intended to make the car purely for his own use, but his friend

Robin Montgomerie-Charrington persuaded him to make a second car and they both took part in Formula 2 races during 1952. The basic car was effective enough, but the Butterworth engine was under-developed and rather unreliable, as well as having insufficient power to deal with Bristol, Gordini, Maserati and Ferrari opposition. Even Gordini was beyond the reach of the Aston-Butterworth cars, so after only one season the project was abandoned and the cars gradually passed into limbo and became disassembled, which is the quickest way for a car to disappear, although one of them has survived through the years, owned by a VSCC member.

Aston Martin

The Aston Martin firm built pure racing cars in the 1920s, their 4-cylinder 16-valve, twin OHC, 1500 cc cars being quite successful. Although the firm pursued an active sports-car racing programme through the 1930s and in the post-war David Brown era, it was not until 1955 that a single-seater Aston Martin racing car appeared from the factory. This was based on a 2.9-litre DB3S sports car and was built for the Australian and New Zealand races of 1955–56. A project to build a car for World Championship Formula 1 racing was started, but progress was slow, due to the racing department concentrating on sports-car racing. The Formula 1, or Grand Prix car, did not appear until 1959, even though the first one had run on test in 1957. By the time it raced the revolutionary change to tiny mid-engined cars, prompted by Cooper, was well under way, so that the front-engined Aston Martin DBR4 was something of a 'dinosaur'. The 6-cylinder engine was of similar design to the sports-car engines, but reduced to 2½ litres capacity, and the chassis and suspension were designed with knowledge gained with the successful DBR1 sports cars.

Three cars were built for the 1959 season, DBR4/1 being driven by Roy Salvadori and DBR4/2 by Carroll Shelby, both drivers having much experience with Aston Martin sports cars. The third car was completed by September 1959, and appeared in the Italian Grand Prix at Monza, driven by Salvadori. Before the end of the season a fourth car was completed, but it was never raced by the works team.

For the 1960 season two new cars were built with improved suspension, smaller chassis frame and more powerful engines and they were overall much lighter. These were DBR5/1 and DBR5/2, driven by Maurice Trintigant and Roy Salvadori, respectively. This was the last season of the 2½-litre Formula, so the DBR5

43

cars had a very short life, both cars being scrapped by the factory after the season was over. Put simply, the single-seater Formula 1 Aston Martins were too big, too heavy, and too late. Had they appeared in 1954 they could well have matched the 250F Maserati Formula 1 car, but even that successful design had been eclipsed the year before the DBR4 first appeared. Had the DBR5 appeared in 1959 it might have had one successful season.

Four DBR4 cars were built, and only two DBR5 cars, and as the DBR5 cars were broken up and scrapped by the factory, historically we can only support four single-seater Aston Martins. The factory team used only three of these in Grand Prix events, and only DBR4/3 is still in existence, on display in the Donington Collection after a complete rebuild, which included a brand new body. Numbers 1 and 2 were broken up, but both have been 'reincarnated', number 1 from some surviving bits and pieces, and number 2 from new and non-racing parts. As a certain amount of original parts went into the 'reconstruction' of DBR4/1 it is accepted by the Aston Martin Owners Club, but the second car has been constructed from scratch and is only acceptable as a 'Facsimile' of the original car. The fourth DBR4, which the factory never raced in Grand Prix events, was sold with a 3-litre sport-car engine installed for use in Australian and New Zealand Tasman racing and the short-lived Inter-Continental Formula racing. After an active career in Australasia it returned to the UK and has been raced fairly regularly in VSCC and Historic racing, at all times in Tasman form with a 3-litre engine.

History

A total of six cars was built; there was no 'prototype' or 'pilot-build' or 'mock-up' of any of these cars. Four were DBR4 series cars and two were DBR5 series cars. Three were officially scrapped by the racing department, so only three can remain and only two of these can be considered to be 'Genuine', the other two in existence being a 'reconstruction' and a 'Facsimile'.

Carroll Shelby at the wheel of Aston Martin DBR4/2 on the model's debut in the 1959 International Trophy at Silverstone. (T. C. March)

DBR4/1   'Reconstructed'
          1959 First appeared at International Trophy at Silverstone driven by
                Roy Salvadori. At end of season this car was dismantled by the
                racing department.
          1960 The chassis was sold to Lex Davidson as spares for DBR4/4.
          1975 Resurrected and 'Reconstructed' using some surviving parts,
                with new chassis frame.
          1978 Bought by Geoffrey Marsh and raced for him in Historic events
                by Richard Bond, Gerry Marshall and Mike Salmon.
          1987 Still owned by Geoffrey Marsh.
DBR4/2   'Scrapped'
          1959 First appeared at International Trophy at Silverstone driven by
                Carroll Shelby.
          1961 Broken up by racing department and scrapped. Chassis frame
                could have been utilized in earlier building of DBR5/2.
DBR4/3   'Genuine'
          1959 First appeared at Italian GP driven by Roy Salvadori.
          1960 Used by works team. At end of season it was fitted with 3-litre
                engine (RB6/300/7) and sold to Bib Stillwell for Tasman racing.
          1966 Returned to UK. Raced by Peter Brewer in VSCC events.
          1970 Restored and re-bodied by Tom Wheatcroft for the Donington
                Racing Car Museum.
          1986 On display in the Donington Collection.
DBR4/4   'Genuine'
          1959 Built by factory as a spare car, but not raced.
          1960 3-litre engine (RB6/300/1) installed and sold to Lex Davidson
                for Tasman racing.
          1968 Returned to UK. Raced by Neil Corner in VSCC and Historic
                racing.
          1978 Bought by Alain de Cadenet. Raced in VSCC and Historic
                racing. Engine badly blown up. Another 3-litre engine installed.
          1985 Bought by Murray Smith.
DBR4   'Facsimile'
          Constructed by Geoffrey Marsh from newly made parts and modified
          production parts in 1979. Sold to John Pearson in 1985.
DBR5/1   'Scrapped'
          1960 First appeared at International Trophy at Silverstone driven by
                Maurice Trintignant.
          1961 Broken up and scrapped by factory.
DBR5/2   'Scrapped'
          1960 First appeared at British GP at Silverstone fitted with indepen-
                dent rear suspension in contrast to the de Dion layout of all pre-
                vious cars. Driven by Roy Salvadori.
          1961 Broken up and scrapped by factory.

Acknowledgements to: Aston Martin Owners Club Registrar; *Historic Racing Cars in Australia* by John Blanden; Brian Joselyne, Neil Corner and Doug Nye.

Austin

Through the enthusiasm of Sir Herbert Austin the Austin Motor Company of Longbridge operated a very active racing department in the twenties and thirties. They competed in the 750 cc class of racing, hill-climbing, sprints and record-breaking. Early racing 750 cc Austins were developed from the original Austin 7 production car, with its tiny 4-cylinder side-valve engine. Some serious supercharging gave the little Sevens a remarkable turn of speed and eventually the stripped sports car gave way to proper single-seater racing cars. This enthusiasm of Sir Herbert culminated in the building of a team of special single-seater 750 cc cars, with supercharged 4-cylinder twin overhead camshaft engines that were truly scaled-down Grand Prix cars. From 1936 to 1939 the Austin 'twin cams', as they were known, were a feature of British racing, as well as some continental events, and were so impressive for their size that everyone lamented that Austin would not build a proper Formula Grand Prix car, or at least a 1500 cc 'voiturette' for International racing. Sir Herbert could not be persuaded, as he wanted to retain an identity between his special racing cars and his production Austin Sevens.

Three of the 'twin cam' cars were built, of which two remain, the third being scrapped after an accident in a hill-climb in 1938. Of the two remaining cars one has been put into running order by the Donington Collection, while the other remains a static exhibit. The last race for the 'twin cams' was at the Crystal Palace in August 1939, when Bert Hadley won the Imperial Trophy race. They never raced again.

Just before the 'twin cams' were built the Austin racing department had reached the limit of development of the supercharged side-valve 750 cc engines and had two slim little single-seaters, one being used for long-distance races and the other

Pat Driscoll with the works supercharged side-valve Austin 7 at the Fork hairpin on the Mountain Circuit at Brooklands in 1935. (The Geoffrey Goddard Collection)

Bert Hadley with the twin overhead camshaft Austin 7 at Donington Park in 1938. (The Author's Collection)

for sprints and hill-climbs. The long-distance version was run in conjunction with the new 'twin cam' cars, but was written-off in a bad crash at Brooklands in 1937. The engine and gearbox were salvaged and kept at the works, but many years later they were 'spirited' away and a homemade copy of the original car was fabricated, though not very accurate in detail, and the original engine and gearbox were installed. It is now a regular competitor in VSCC events. The remaining works side-valve car has survived the years and has been put into running order by the Donington Collection, and can be seen on display alongside its sophisticated 'twin cam' brother.

History

Side-valve No. 1 — 'Scrapped'. Badly damaged in accident at Brooklands in 1937 when driven by Mrs. K. Petre. Engine and gearbox salvaged, rest of car scrapped.

Side-valve No. 2 — 'Genuine'. Retained by the Austin Motor Company. Passed on to BMC, British Leyland, and BL Heritage. Restored to running order by the Donington Collection in 1974 and on display in the museum.

Twin cam No. 1 — 'Scrapped'. Badly damaged in accident at Backwell hill-climb in 1938. Scrapped by factory.

Twin cam No. 2 — 'Genuine'. Last raced by the Austin Motor Company in 1939, driven by Charlie Dodson. Restored to running order by the Donington Collection in 1974 and on display in the museum.

Twin cam No. 3 — 'Genuine'. Last raced by the Austin Motor Company in 1939, driven by Bert Hadley. Retained as non-running exhibition car by British Leyland Heritage.

Side-valve 'F' — 'Facsimile'. Built by Peter Moores. Only the engine and gearbox are original and genuine.

Acknowledgements to H. L. Hadley and The Donington Collection.

Auto Union

Auto Union AG was a consortium of four German automobile firms who joined forces during the depression years of the early thirties, before the Third Reich took over in 1933. These firms were Audi, Wanderer, D.K.W. and Horch, and they adopted a badge made up of four interlinked rings, with the name Auto Union across them.

Encouraged to go motor racing by the new Nazi Government, Auto Union purchased a design for a Grand Prix car from Dr. Ferdinand Porsche in 1933 in readiness for the new Grand Prix Formula due to start in 1934. They also employed him as their chief engineer for the racing department. Dr. Porsche's design was revolutionary and far-seeing in 1933, for today most Grand Prix cars have an identical layout. The driving position was well forward, the fuel tank and engine being behind the driver, and the 5-speed gearbox stuck out the back behind the rear axle. The engine was a V-16 cylinder unit supercharged by a large single blower and the suspension was independent to all four wheels, by torsion bars at the front and a transverse leaf spring at the rear; brakes were hydraulically operated. Auto Union was one of the major contestants in Grand Prix racing between 1934 and 1939, covering the 750 kilogram Formula 1934 to 1937 and the 3-litre class of the Formula 1938 to 1940.

The original P-Wagen was developed through three series, A, B and C, with changes to engine capacity, rear suspension, bodywork, superchargers and shock absorbers. The engine capacity grew from 4.3 litres to 6.1 litres, always retaining the V-16 layout and the intricate valve gear operating all 32 valves from one central camshaft using short pushrods and rockers. It developed prodigious torque at fairly low rpm and with the major weight mass at the rear its traction and acceleration were outstanding. The drawback was 'tail-happy' handling that called for some finesse in keeping the car under control. The rear suspension was changed from the original transverse leaf spring to longitudinal torsion bars, but the swing-axle geometry was retained. The C-type Auto Union was the ultimate development of the P-Wagen and holds the distinction of having won the last race to be run under the 750 kilogram Formula, which was the 1937 Donington Park Grand Prix.

By 1938 the Auto Union racing department was taken over by Prof. Dr. Ing. Eberan von Eberhorst, who had been Porsche's assistant in the days of the 16-cylinder cars. He designed an entirely new car for the new formula, using a V-12

The 6-litre V-16 Auto Union of Herman Müller in the Coppa Acerbo at Pescara in 1937.
(The Geoffrey Goddard Collection)

This 3-litre V-12 D-type Auto Union is seen driven by Rudolf Hasse in the Donington Grand Prix in 1938. (The Geoffrey Goddard Collection)

cylinder layout, with three overhead camshafts and provision for the development of high-pressure supercharging by a two-stage system. The driving seat was moved rearwards by moving some of the fuel tank capacity into pannier tanks alongside the cockpit. Chassis frame and front suspension followed the C-type design, but the rear suspension was changed from independent to de Dion layout.

In 1939 the two-stage supercharging layout was adopted and the D-type Auto Union won the last Formula Grand Prix race to be held, before war put a stop to racing. This was in Belgrade on the day that England declared war on Germany, 3 September, 1939. In addition to the teams of A-, B-, C- and D-type Auto Unions the firm also participated in numerous record attempts with special 'Rekord-wagen'.

After the war Auto Union AG was split up between East and West Germany, Audi and D.K.W. being in the West, while Horch and Wanderer were in the East, and no Auto Union racing department was re-formed. The majority of the pre-war material was destroyed in the bombing of Germany and only a few items survived.

For many years after the war all traces of the great Auto Union racing team seemed to have been wiped off the face of the earth. The only tangible proof that it ever existed lay in photographs and an exhibition car, with sectioned bodywork, in the Deutsches Museum in Munich. But for this museum car, one would have begun to wonder if the Auto Union racing team had ever existed!

After many years, rumours began to spread about an Auto Union in Czechoslovakia, and eventually this 'mythical' Auto Union became reality, and it was winkled out of the East and passed into the West in 1974. It was found to be a 1938 car that had been built up as an exhibition car for the Berlin Motor Show. There was no crankshaft, connecting rods or pistons in the engine, nor any internals in the gearbox. The crankshaft assembly, which was a fully roller-bearing unit, built up on the Hirth patents, was on display in a technical museum in Moscow. While the chassis and bodywork were overhauled in England, a complete engine unit was 'found' in the east zone of Germany, and spirited out. An English journalist concocted an absurd story that it had been found near Donington Park, said to have been left behind after the Grand Prix in 1938! It was a two-stage 1939 engine that was soon got into working order and installed in the 1938 chassis. The gearbox was replaced by a modified English Hewland gearbox/axle unit, and the car was made to run. It is now owned by one of England's foremost Historic Racing Car enthusiasts and has been properly restored to full running order.

Meanwhile, an old-car gathering was held in Riga and a V-16 Auto Union was produced. It was not in working order, but was undoubtedly a C-type, used for hill-climbs by the factory team in 1939, and had been borrowed from a Moscow museum, where it had been since the end of the war. This was the first sign of any Auto Union cars existing in Russia.

The great interest in Auto Union racing prompted the Audi–N.S.U. firm to take a closer look at the car in the Munich museum. It was a feasible project to restore it to working order and complete it. This was done at the N.S.U. factory and the whole restoration project was undertaken as only an engineering concern like N.S.U. could hope to achieve. It was shown to the world in 1980 and made demonstration runs before being put back into the Deutsches Museum in Munich. There was no intention to participate in Historic Racing, but it is taken out and demonstrated on very special occasions. That Audi–N.S.U. have restored this car to full working order is something for which racing enthusiasts everywhere will be eternally grateful.

Known cars:

C-type–1936–37 'Genuine'. Restored and completed by Audi–N.S.U. in 1979–80 into a fully working car. On display in the Deutsches Museum in Munich.
C-type–1937–39 'Genuine'. Hill-climb car, unrestored, in Latvia.
D-type–1938–39 'Authentic'. 1938 chassis with 1939 two-stage supercharged engine unit, built up in England. Restored 1974 to 1986.

Acknowledgements to *Auto Union Grand Prix Wagen* by Stefan Knittel, *Motor Sport*, December 1982.

Auto Union/D.A.M.W./A.W.E.

This car surfaced in the late 1970s in East Germany and found its way to the UK to join Tom Wheatcroft's Donington Collection. When it arrived it was incomplete, with no vestiges of bodywork, and had clearly never been driven under its own power, though the engine had obviously run at some time. Its origins at the time of arrival in the UK were obscure, to say the least, though some myths and suggestions came with the car, few of which withstood close scrutiny.

Subsequent research by various people in Germany and England filled in enough to produce a reasonable story, but it is only circumstantial. There was a lot of Auto Union about the design of the chassis, but the engine was very much 'state-of-the-art' of around 1950, as was much of the transmission and rear end of the car.

It seems to have been built by a group of engineers who probably came from the pre-war Auto Union racing department, and though built with limited resources and finances, it was well engineered and not a 'back-yard special'. The unsupercharged 2-litre V-12 engine, with four overhead camshafts, would suggest that it was built for the Formula 2 that was in operation in 1950, at the time when Germany was being allowed back into International racing. Research suggested that the constructors of the engine had no test facilities, so took it to the racing department of D.A.M.W., which was situated in the old B.M.W. factories at Eisenach.

The *Deutsches Amt Für Material und Warenprufung*, which produced the E.M.W. cars and became the Automobile Werke Eisenach (A.W.E.) that raced very interesting 2-litre sports cars, tested the V-12 engine and more or less took over the project, but it never saw a racing circuit. How it left the Eisenach works is

The Auto Union/D.A.M.W. 2-litre chassis on arrival at Tilbury Docks in December 1978.
(The Geoffrey Goddard Collection)

anyone's guess, but it certainly arrived at Tilbury Docks and was taken to Donington Park. The firm of Hall & Fowler, at Folkingham, did a superb job in dismantling the engine, making new parts for those they found broken, and got the whole thing working, completing the chassis and running gear. It was clothed with a bodywork based on some 1950 pictures reproduced in a German magazine, and gave demonstration runs at Donington Park.

The body was painted silver in the style of pre-war Auto Unions, and it was given an Auto Union four-ring insignia on the nose, which was not exactly correct, and it should have had D.A.M.W. or A.W.E. on the nose. Some people like to think that it represents a 1940 Auto Union E-type, but this is wishful thinking, for close inspection of the design and mechanical details makes this theory most unlikely.

It is certainly an interesting single-seater racing car of Grand Prix aspect and well qualified to take its place in the Donington Racing Car Museum.

B.R.M. V-16

The V-16 B.R.M. has had more words written about it than most Grand Prix cars, and certainly the words-to-success ratio has never been surpassed. On paper the car was a fascinating *tour de force* of engineering, but in fact it was beyond the technical capabilities of those in charge and it ended up as one of the greatest Grand Prix failures, if not the greatest.

The firm of British Racing Motors was created by Raymond Mays and designer Peter Berthon, and after gaining limited financial support from the British motor industry the project was very slow in getting under way. Though it started in 1945 it was 1950 before a V-16 B.R.M. appeared on a starting line. From the committee of sponsors that were trying to run the team, Sir Alfred Owen and his Industrial Group took over control, and floundered their way through the 1951 season of Grand Prix racing without making any impression, apart from a bad one, and, when the Grand Prix Formula changed at the beginning of 1952, principally due to B.R.M.'s inability to commit itself to a serious International programme of races, the V-16 Formula 1 cars became obsolete.

Thereafter, B.R.M. continued development of the cars, producing a Mark 2 Formule Libre version, and were strong supporters of British National racing, not

much above club level. At this low level of competition the B.R.M. made an impression, and left behind the memorable sound of the supercharged V-16 engine exhausting through short stub pipes.

Three Mark 1 cars were built, the outward shape and design changing from an impractical svelt profile to an unseemly untidy shape full of holes and louvres and air intakes, much needed to keep the car cool. The three Mark 1 cars were driven by Reg Parnell, Peter Walker, Stirling Moss, Juan Fangio, Ken Wharton and Froilan Gonzalez, so it could not be said that they lacked talent behind the wheel. In the 1953 Albi non-Formula race Ken Wharton had a high-speed accident, from which he escaped, but the car was a complete write-off and was scrapped. In 1954 at the Easter meeting at Goodwood, Wharton wrote off another Mark 1 B.R.M. when he was rammed by Roy Salvadori in a 250F Maserati, the impact bending the chassis frame severely, though the car kept going and actually won the short sprint-race. As the shorter and lighter Mark 2 B.R.M. was now running, there was little point in repairing the Mark 1, so it was scrapped.

The Mark 2 cars, of which two were built, used the same V-16 supercharged engines, gearboxes and suspensions, but were trimmed down for the small National events that the team were supporting. Had the supercharged 1½-litre Formula still been in existence the Mark 2 cars would not have been able to take part as they were essentially 'sprint' cars, rather than Grand Prix cars. Wharton, Ron Flockhart and Peter Collins raced the Mark 2 cars, but the end of the life of the V-16 cars was in sight as B.R.M. had started work on an unsupercharged 2½-litre design for the new Formula that came into being in 1954.

The B.R.M. cars and equipment were put up for auction in 1981, and the sole remaining Grand Prix type Mark 1, which had been kept by Rubery Owen for demonstration purposes, went to a collector, but subsequently was acquired by the Beaulieu National Motor Museum. One of the Mark 2 cars had always been kept in running order, and had given demonstration runs at various times, and this was acquired by Tom Wheatcroft for his Donington Collection. The second Mark 2 car was loosely assembled, but was incomplete, and after being acquired by an anonymous collector it passed into the hands of Rock drummer Nick Mason, who has had it rebuilt and completed for use in Historic racing.

For 1954 B.R.M. produced the lighter, shorter Mk II version of the V-16; Ron Flockhart is seen here in the Richmond Trophy at Goodwood on Easter Monday. (LAT)

History

A complex centrifugally supercharged 1½-litre V-16 cylinder engine in a chassis and suspension based on the 'state-of-the-art' of 1939, even though the car was designed in 1945–47. Three Mark 1 cars built for the works team; two crashed and scrapped. Two Mark 2 versions built, using the same mechanical components, tailored to short-circuit National racing. Both have survived. Until the liquidation Auction Sale in 1981 the B.R.M. cars were strictly works machines, neither loaned nor sold to anybody outside the works team.

B.R.M. Mark 1	Car number one. The only survivor of the the team, on display in the National Motor Museum. 'Genuine.'
B.R.M. Mark 1	Car number two. Written off by the factory after Ken Wharton's accident at Albi. 'Scrapped.'
B.R.M. Mark 1	Car number three. Broken up by the factory after the chassis was badly bent in an accident at Goodwood. 'Scrapped.'
B.R.M. Mark 2	Built in 1954 using the mechanical components from the Mark 1 cars. In the Donington Collection. 'Genuine.'
B.R.M. Mark 2	Built in 1954 using the mechanical components from the Mark 1 cars. In Historic racing. 'Genuine.'

Acknowledgements to B.R.M. Archives, Doug Nye.

B.R.M. P25

After the extravagance and complication of the V-16 B.R.M. cars the firm made a complete reversal with their next project. This was the P25 model designed for the 1954–1960 Grand Prix Formula, with 2½-litre unsupercharged engine. It was simple, small, straightforward and uncomplicated and though late in coming on the Grand Prix scene, and suffering too many 'teething' troubles, it did feature strongly during most of the life of the Formula. All too often it looked like a winner, only to fail, and apart from some minor victories it only achieved one win in a World Championship Grand Prix. This was the Dutch Grand Prix of 1959, when Jo Bonnier drove to victory.

In total, B.R.M. built 11 cars in the P25 series and they were to be the last front-engined cars to come from the Bourne factory; by the end of the Formula, in 1960, a revolution had taken place in Grand Prix car design, prompted more by rule changes and expediency than basic concepts, and B.R.M. lost no time in joining the revolution.

The P25 cars were built in two series, the first five cars with a stressed-skin cockpit area, and the next six with a complete space-frame of small-diameter tubing. The first series were fast but fragile and it is interesting, and probably significant, that the first four cars were written off in lurid accidents in the three seasons 1956–58; fortunately none of the drivers was seriously hurt. The fifth car was broken up and useful bits were put into the spares store for the 1959 team cars.

It was one of the second series cars that achieved B.R.M.'s only World Championship Grand Prix victory in the era of front-engined cars from 1950 until 1960. The penultimate P25, number 10, was loaned in 1959 to Stirling Moss and his father's private racing team, known as the British Racing Partnership (B.R.P.), but even then outright victory eluded them and the car was ultimately written off in a violent crash at the Avus circuit while being driven by Hans Herrmann. Four remaining second series cars were broken up and cannibalized to make the prototypes of the rear-engined P48 cars, and one original P25 survived, thought to be the actual Dutch Grand Prix winner, though some people dispute this.

With the advent of the rear-engined era of Grand Prix racing the old-fashioned

The 2½-litre B.R.M. was by the standards of its contemporaries small, squat and very powerful – but persistently unreliable. Tony Brooks is at the wheel in the 1956 British Grand Prix in which he crashed badly when the throttle jammed open. (T. C. March)

front-engined saga was forgotten until the 1970s, when Tom Wheatcroft decided he would like a P25 B.R.M. in his Donington Collection. The sole remaining car was still at the Bourne factory, but was not for sale, so he searched around as far afield as Australia and found the derelict remains of some of the P48 rear-engined cars that had been created from the remnants of the broken-up P25 cars. Starting with B.R.M.'s blessing, he made brand new chassis frames to the P25 drawings, and his workshops reconstructed three cars, using original B.R.M. engines, gear-boxes, brakes, wheels and suspension parts, but with new bodies, tanks, and detail parts. With B.R.M.'s agreement he gave the cars original works chassis numbers, one of them being 2510, the car crashed at Avus, as he had found some mangled remains from the wreckage. About the same time a fourth car was reconstructed, claiming connection with the last of the 'stressed-skin' cars, though it was built in the form of a second series car, so it can only be considered a 'Facsimile'.

One of the three Donington Collection cars was used in Historic racing, driven by Neil Corner, and it was very successful, though it had to use a lot of spare parts taken from the other two cars to keep it mobile.

When B.R.M. went into liquidation and the contents of the factory were sold by auction, the sole remaining genuine P25 was acquired by VSCC members, and is unique in Historic racing in being the only real P25, built at Bourne by B.R.M. in 1958.

History

Eleven cars.were built at Bourne for the works racing team, five first series cars, of which none survived and six second series cars of which one survived. The three cars 'reconstructed' by the Donington Collection have taken original chassis num-bers, and there is a fourth car which is a 'Facsimile' and is a mixture of first and second series design. At the B.R.M. factory the engines took the Project Number 25, and the chassis frames were Project Number 27, while the complete cars took serial numbers prefixed with 25.

Chassis No. 25/1	Works car 1955–58. Written off by Ron Flockhart in crash at Silverstone in 1958. 'Scrapped.'
Chassis No. 25/2	Works car 1956. Written off by Tony Brooks at Silver-stone in 1956. 'Scrapped.'

Stirling Moss on his way to second place in the 1959 British Grand Prix at Aintree with the light green P25 loaned to the British Racing Partnership. (T. C. March)

Chassis No. 25/3	Works car 1956–58. Written off by Jean Behra in crash at Goodwood in 1958. 'Scrapped.'
Chassis No. 25/4	Works car 1957–58. Written off by Ron Flockhart in a crash at Rouen in 1957. 'Scrapped.'
Chassis No. 25/5	Works car broken up to provide spares for 1959 team cars.
Chassis No. 25/6	Works car 1958–59. Broken up to provide spares for P48 cars.
Chassis No. 25/7	Works car 1958–59. Broken up to provide spares for P48 cars 'Reconstructed' by Donington Collection.
Chassis No. 25/8	Only remaining P25 built by B.R.M.: works car 1958–59/60. Now in private hands.
Chassis No. 25/9	Works car 1958–59. Broken up. Useful parts into works team P48 spares pool. 'Reconstructed' by Donington Collection.
Chassis No. 25/10	Works car 1959. Crashed at Avus by Herrmann. Written off. 'Reconstructed' by Donington Collection.
Chassis No. 25/11	Works car 1959–60. Broken up. Useful parts into works team P48 spares pool.

Acknowledgements to: B.R.M. Archives; Doug Nye, *Autosport* 22 October, 1981.

Ballot

Before the First World War the Ballot firm were making engines for industrial and commercial use by other people, but once the war was over Monsieur Ballot decided to go into car manufacture himself. To launch the idea he planned an audacious entry into motor racing, seeing it as a good medium to establish himself in the motoring world. He engaged the services of the Swiss designer Ernest Henry, who had made a great name for Peugeot, and at very short notice decided to enter for the Indianapolis 500 Mile race due to be run in May 1919. Henry was to design, and Ballot to build, a series of cars that were to set the design fashion in racing engines and racing cars for many years to come. The 1919 Ballot racing cars had straight-eight-cylinder engines, with two overhead camshafts, 4-valves per cylinder, twin carburettors and a capacity of 4.9 litres. The chassis was equally advanced, being long and low, though the bodywork was reminiscent of cars of the Edwardian era, with two seats and a bolster-type fuel tank across the rear of the chassis.

Four of these cars were built, given the simple numbering of 1001, 1002, 1003 and 1004, and they ran in the 500 Mile race. They were comfortably the fastest cars on the track in practice. The wheels were changed for some American ones, which were larger and would effectively raise the rear axle ratio, but these gave trouble in the race and the team came home to France empty-handed, their best placing being fourth by Albert Guyot. One of the team made fastest lap at 104.7 mph.

A single car was sent to the Targa Florio in 1920, but it retired with a broken

The Ballot Straight Eight 5-litre at Indianapolis in 1919. At the wheel is René Thomas. (Guy Griffiths)

back axle and in the autumn of that year Jean Chassagne raced one at Brooklands, putting in a lap at 112.17 mph.

For the major international races of 1920, and this included Indianapolis, a limit of 3 litres was imposed on the engines, so Henry started all over again with his design and Ballot produced a team of 3-litre cars almost identical to the previous 5-litre cars, except that the body was improved with a tapering pointed tail in which a spare wheel was carried vertically down the centre of the tail.

Although four cars were built, continuing the number sequence of the 5 litres, 1005, 1006, 1007 and 1008, only the last three ran in the 1920 Indianapolis race. Again they were the fastest cars on the track, and Ralph de Palma was leading until less than 50 miles from the finish, when a fuel leak developed and the car caught fire. The fire was put out, with little damage being done and the car continued, to finish fifth, but meanwhile René Thomas, who had been lying third, moved up to finish second. The third car, driven by Chassagne, finished seventh.

In 1921 the team took part in the French Grand Prix, but were outpaced by the fiery Jimmy Murphy and his Duesenberg. They returned for another go at the Indianapolis 500 Mile race, when Ralph de Palma drove a singleton entry, but retired with engine trouble, having been easily the fastest in qualifying. The 1921 season finished with a glorious first and second in the Italian Grand Prix at Brescia and at that point Edouard Ballot withdrew his eight-cylinder cars from the big-time racing and concentrated on production sports and touring cars, and lesser racing events.

Jules Goux took a pair of the 3-litre cars to Indianapolis in 1922, and though he retired from the race himself, the American driver of the other one finished third. That was the last 3-litre race at Indianapolis, for the following year the capacity limit was reduced to 2 litres, so the only place these fast French cars could run was the Brooklands track and a 3-litre and a 5-litre were both very active at the Surrey track in the mid-twenties, driven by Campbell, Zborowski and Howey, the last

R.B. Howey at the wheel of a 5-litre Ballot re-bodied in 3-litre form at Brooklands in 1922.
(The Geoffrey Goddard Collection)

named eventually lapping at 121.18 mph. The 3-litre was raced until 1932 by Jack Dunfee, and then in the late 1930s it appeared in VSCC racing.

This car has recently reappeared after a very long and meticulous rebuild, which included redesigning the internals of the engine, with new crankshaft, rods, pistons and camshafts to a better and more modern firing order for a straight-eight engine, so that now it is even more powerful and efficient than it was when it was built in 1920.

Only one of the 5-litre cars seems to have survived, and that is in the United States, while there was a 3-litre in the Cunningham Museum in California, and another in the Schlumpf Museum in France.

History

Built by the Ballot factory in Paris, these straight-eight cars designed by Ernest Henry set a standard and fashion that many others were to develop right through to the mid-1950s, Bugatti, Alfa Romeo, Maserati, Mercedes-Benz and Gordini all developing the straight-eight-cylinder layout for Grand Prix cars. The Ballot works team competed in 1919, 1920 and 1921, their best Indianapolis placing being second in 1921, and that year they won the Italian Grand Prix.

Ballot 4.9-litre – Chassis No. 1001 – ⎫
 Chassis No. 1002 – ⎪
 Chassis No. 1003 – ⎬ Untraced.
 Chassis No. 1004 – ⎪
Ballot 3.0-litre – Chassis No. 1005 – ⎭
 Chassis No. 1006 – Rebuilt and owned by Humphrey Milling.
 Chassis No. 1007 – Being restored, Cunningham Museum.
 Chassis No. 1008 – In Schlumpf Museum.

Acknowledgements to: *Motor Sport*, June 1978; *The Grand Prix Car* by Lawrence Pomeroy; *The Indianapolis 500* by Jack C. Fox.

Bentley

The old Bentley Company of Cricklewood in North-West London were renowned for their sports cars, their Le Mans victories and their very high-performance town carriages, as well as for some famous Brooklands activities with stripped sports cars. Long after the firm collapsed and was taken over by Rolls-Royce, the old name of Bentley was kept in the forefront of Brooklands track racing by numerous 'specials' built around Bentley components from the old Cricklewood days, and these went on racing until the track closed in August 1939.

Barnato-Hassan – 'Authentic.' This was the fastest of all the special Bentleys vying for the out-and-out lap record at Brooklands with the 24-litre Napier-Railton. It was constructed by Walter Hassan, who had learnt his trade with the old Bentley company, and it was to the order of Woolf Barnato, one of the old 'Bentley Boys'. Barnato had retired from race driving but had lost none of his enthusiasm, and the Barnato-Hassan was designed specifically for racing on the Brooklands banked track, to be driven by his friends.

It was based on a standard 6½-litre Bentley to start with, a single-seater body being constructed around the offset driving position. Later it was rebuilt into a pure single-seater with a central driving position and a remarkably slim and slippery body. The engine was replaced with an 8-litre Bentley engine and this underwent considerable development, ending up with three enormous SU carburettors fed by a long ram-air duct pointing forwards and with the entry alongside the radiator cowl. This cowl was slimmed down to present the minimum opening, in the form of a tall thin slot, but it passed adequate air to the radiator at speeds of 140 mph and more. The chassis and half-elliptic springs front and rear were all carefully cowled in and a long tail and head-fairing behind the cockpit kept the airflow in good shape right back to the end of the long car.

Driven by Oliver Bertram it was a regular competitor in Outer Circuit Brooklands handicap races, as well as the 500 Mile race, and was one of the star performers until Barnato withdrew it at the end of 1938. This was due to the

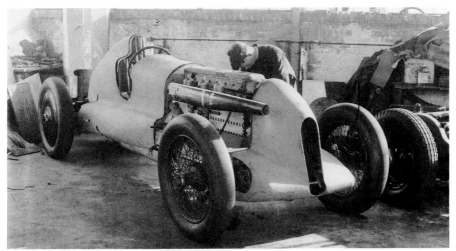

The Barnato-Hassan, owned by Woolf Barnato and driven by Oliver Bertram, seen in 1938 in the Thomson & Taylor workshops at Brooklands. (The Geoffrey Goddard Collection)

'Tim' Birkin in the Blower 4½-litre single-seater Bentley at Brooklands in the 1930 BRDC 500 mile race. (The Geoffrey Goddard Collection)

Brooklands Automobile Racing Club's handicapping system that not only made it virtually impossible for the Barnato–Hassan to win, even though it was lapping close to the lap record in trying, but meant that Bertram was having a pretty dangerous time passing slower cars at the top of the banking.

The pale silvery-blue Barnato-Hassan was the epitome of Brooklands Outer Circuit cars and remained the second fastest car to lap the banked track, its best lap being 143.11 mph during a handicap race in September 1938. The fastest ever lap, by John Cobb in the Napier-Railton, was 143.44 mph.

It was stored safely through the war years, on the assumption that racing would restart on the Brooklands track, but it was not to be, so the car was sold. As it had no possibility of use as a single-seater it was converted into a two-seater sports car, with a bulbous and ugly body that gave it the nickname 'The Whale'. It actually took part in the Spa 24 Hour race in this form, but soon passed into the care of owners in the Bentley Drivers Club and was used in vintage and historic events in contemporary company. Over the years it has had regular moments of intense activity and then a long period of rest, only to appear again, and it has been converted back to a single-seater, but it is not as sleek and purposeful as it was in its heyday of 1937–38.

Birkin Single-seater – 'Genuine.' This special Bentley single-seater is probably the most famous of all special Bentleys, and certainly was the most successful in its day. Sir Henry Birkin, under the patronage of the Hon. Dorothy Paget, instigated the project of supercharging the 4½-litre Bentley engine, even though W. O. Bent-

The 6½-litre Bentley-Jackson seen behind the paddock at Brooklands in 1939. (The Geoffrey Goddard Collection)

ley disapproved. With the aid of Amherst Villiers, a specialist in supercharging and high engine power outputs, Birkin went ahead with supercharged cars for Le Mans and the Tourist Trophy. They were fast, but unsuccessful in terms of race victories, but created a legend for themselves as the 'Blower Bentleys'. Not surprisingly, Birkin built a single-seater version for use on the Brooklands Outer Circuit, even though he professed to dislike such racing and was strong in his criticisms of the Weybridge track. Painted red, the Birkin 'blower' single-seater soon made a name for itself, vying for the lap record of the banked track with cars such as the 4-litre V-12 Sunbeam. By 1932 it held the lap record at 137.96 mph and ended its track life when Sir Henry died in 1933.

It passed into the world of the Vintage Sports Car Club and at one point its engine was used to keep one of the Birkin sports Bentleys on the road. In post-war years it was never lost sight of, and eventually was rebuilt and given the minimum of road-equipment so that it could be driven about as a sports car, even though the body was still the original offset single-seater. It has stayed in appreciative hands within the Bentley Drivers Club for many years, and now lives in the Isle of Man, but makes frequent trips to the mainland for Vintage and Historic events.

Bentley-Jackson – 'Genuine.' This was another special Bentley that evolved from a normal 6½-litre car. The work was carried out by Robin Jackson at his premises behind the Brooklands Paddock for Richard Marker. It began as an offset single-seater, but by 1938 it had become a central driving position pure single-seater, with an aerodynamically designed body in aluminium. It may have been aerodynamically functional, but it was not a very pretty car and looked far bigger than it really was. R. R. K. Marker drove it regularly in Outer Circuit Brooklands races, as did George Harvey-Noble and C. T. Baker-Carr.

It was never fast enough to challenge for the outright lap record at Brooklands, but could always be guaranteed to put in laps around the 130 mph mark, its best being 134.97 mph in 1938.

Like all the Brooklands Outer Circuit track cars, it found itself obsolete in 1946. It actually made an appearance at the Brighton Speed Trials at one point, but basically it did not get used again, though it remains in the keeping of a member of the Bentley Drivers Club.

The Pacey-Hassan Bentley Special built by Walter Hassan for E. W. W. Pacey and seen at Brooklands in 1937. (The Geoffrey Goddard Collection)

Pacey-Hassan – 'Authentic.' This was another special Bentley built for Brooklands Outer Circuit racing by Wally Hassan. It was to the order of E. W. W. Pacey, who raced sports Bentleys, and was constructed around 4½-litre Bentley components, on a specially designed chassis frame, underslung at the rear, which Rubery Owen made for Hassan. Naturally the shape and style of the body was very similar to the Barnato-Hassan and it was painted black. It first appeared in 1936 and Pacey raced it fairly regularly but with little success, the unsupercharged 4½-litre engine not providing sufficient power to match the speed of 6½-litre and 8-litre cars.

After the war it disappeared into the Bentley Drivers Club firmament and some years ago was entirely rebuilt, still as a single-seater, but with the addition of front-wheel brakes and smaller-diameter wheels, as the intention was to use it in Vintage racing, which indeed the present owner still does.

Benz

Carl Benz, who started the automobile industry 100 years ago, was not a great believer in competitions and racing, though two of his cars finished second and third in the 1908 Grand Prix. He did, however, build some very powerful cars intended for Grand Touring and the 21½-litre 4-cylinder 'Blitzen' model was raced by owners, and even modified into out-and-out racing and record-breaking cars.

One of these big 4-cylinder Benz cars came to England and did a lot of racing at the Brooklands track in the early 1920s. It was later fitted with a four-seater touring body and used for Grand Touring, which was the original intention behind the

The 200 hp Benz Blitzen at Silverstone in April 1949. (Guy Griffiths)

design. It was active in VSCC racing for a while, but eventually time caught up with it and it retired to the Birmingham Museum of Science and Industry, where it can be seen today. Another 'Blitzen' Benz in racing form is kept in the Daimler-Benz museum in Stuttgart.

In 1923, from the designs of Dr Rumpler, the Benz factory produced some revolutionary Grand Prix cars for the 2-litre Formula. Known as the 'Tropfenwagen' (tear-drop-car) this design had a 6-cylinder engine mounted amidships, behind the driving cockpit and ahead of the rear axle. A streamlined header tank and water radiator were mounted above the engine, protruding from the bodywork. This allowed the front of the car to be a bullet-shaped cowling devoid of openings, a most desirable feature aerodynamically. Front suspension was by a beam axle on ¼-elliptic leaf springs, but at the rear the wheels were sprung independently on swinging half-axles, again with ¼-elliptic springs. The chassis frame was of channel-section steel and copiously drilled to reduce weight and the aluminium body was very smooth and streamlined, with a long, pointed tail.

The life of the 'Tropfenwagen' in International racing was very short, and not very sweet, with a single appearance in the 1923 Italian Grand Prix at Monza. In addition to the single-seater racing versions, a two-seater road-equipped sports version was made, but the whole project was very short-lived. None of the cars survived, though there was one still running in hill-climbs in Rumania as late as 1950; so who knows, it may still be lurking in the cellars of a tractor factory!

It is interesting that when Benz merged with Mercedes in 1926 to form Mercedes-Benz, there was no sign of the Rumpler design being resurrected in Stuttgart, even though Ferdinand Porsche, who was working for Daimler-Benz, had been a pupil of Dr Rumpler. In 1933, from his own design studio, Porsche produced the mid-engined Grand Prix car that was to become the Auto Union, a direct descendant of the 'Tropfenwagen'.

The 1923 Benz 'Tropfenwagen'. (The Geoffrey Goddard Collection)

Bolster Special 1

This special personifies the title 'home made.' It was built by John Bolster on his mother's farm in Kent during the early 1930s and its execution was definitely agricultural. It compromised a simple frame into which two V-twin 1000 cc J.A.P. motorcycle engines were fitted. They were mounted slightly to the left, one behind the other and their main-shafts were joined by chain. From the rear engine another chain took the drive to a motorcycle gearbox and clutch, and a further chain drove to the rear axle.

The driver sat very low within the frame, alongside the chain drive, and to the right of the car, his right arm being outside the chassis frame, necessitating a short piece of mudguard over the right rear wheel to protect his elbow.

In speed trials and hill-climbs the Bolster Special, known affectionately as 'Bloody Mary', was always one of the faster and more spectacular performers, its tiny size belying the 2 litres of alcohol-burning J.A.P. power under the low bonnet. The engines were air-cooled and a cut-down G.N. radiator shell was used to carry the engine cover and to pass air through to the engines. Suspension was by quarter-elliptic leaf springs and was basically G.N.

For a brief period in 1938–39 'Bloody Mary' lay fallow as the engines were re-moved, to be fitted along with two more similar units, into a fiercesome four-engined 4-litre Bolster Special, on similar lines. It boasted such sophistication as independent front suspension and hydraulic brakes, and was intended for circuit racing in addition to sprints and hill-climbs. The war cut short its development, for development was needed to get four V-twin engines, joined together by driving chains, running in unison.

After the war John Bolster resurrected 'Bloody Mary' re-installing her two engines, and he then used her in sprints, hill-climbs and VSCC events, until he retired from racing. She was put on display in the National Motor Museum at Beaulieu as a prime example of the home-built Special Builder's art and she remains as a fitting tribute to John Bolster, a great enthusiast and accomplished driver, as well as a forthright journalist in his later years. Sadly John Bolster died in 1980, but 'Bloody Mary' will live on.

John Bolster at the wheel of 'Bloody Mary' at Silverstone in May, 1953. (Guy Griffiths)

Bolster Special 2

Special building was part of life in the Bolster family, and elder brother Richard was as inventive as younger brother John. Their mother used a Colmore Frazer Nash as her everyday car, so it was not surprising that chain-drive came naturally to the brothers and early G.N.s formed the basis for their specials.

Richard's car was a bit more conventional than 'Bloody Mary', having a central driving seat and fairly orthodox-looking single-seater body. However, underneath it was as ingenious and as complicated as John's car. Richard mounted four Rudge motorcycle engines in-line and coupled them together with chains, the last chain driving to a motorcycle gearbox and another chain running back to the rear axle, all this down the left side of the chassis.

The big problem was synchronizing the four single-cylinder engines, but when they did decide to run in unison they gave quite a lethal amount of power from their total of 2 litres, each air-cooled unit being of 499 cc. Eventually Richard gave up the unequal struggle and replaced them with a conventional automobile power unit. This was a 1100 cc 6-cylinder M.G. Magnette engine, with an M.G. gearbox coupled to a Frazer Nash bevel-box and cross-shaft to give chain final-drive to the solid back axle. An early Talbot-Darracq radiator was used to cool the M.G. engine, and in this form Richard was able to compete in short racing events, such as Club meetings at Donington Park.

Richard lost his life flying with the RAF during the war, but remarkably his Special survived, though it was not used. In recent years it has been resurrected by a VSCC member and is back in use in all manner of Vintage events.

The Richard Bolster special. (Rodger McDonald)

Bugatti 'Brescia'

The Bugatti Owners Club bracket three Bugatti models together, under the heading 16-valve. These are the Types 13, 22 and 23 and all are 4-cylinder models, with a single overhead camshaft and four valves per cylinder. They all had a stroke of 100 mm, but the bore came in three sizes, 66, 68 and 69 mm, giving three capacities of 1368, 1453 and 1496 cc. The period of manufacture of this trio of Bugatti models is quoted as 1914 to 1926, with a total production of 2000. After these little cars had performed well in the Italian event at Brescia in 1921, this name was used for the 16-valve sporting cars from Molsheim.

With such a large production run of what was obviously a very popular sporting car, it is surprising that so few have survived intact. Many bits and pieces have been discovered over the years, especially in recent times, and being a comparatively simple design, it has been an easy matter to construct 'Facsimiles' around a basic component such as an engine or a back axle. With so many cars being built originally it hardly matters how many 'Facsimiles' are made these days, provided the total does not exceed 2000!

As an exciting little vintage sports car the 16-valve Bugatti provides a lot of harmless fun and is very popular in VSCC trials and driving tests. Of the many that are so active, all have some trace of Molsheim about them, the content varying from 5 per cent in the case of 'new' ones, to 90 per cent in the case of genuine ones, but all are equally pleasing and have little effect on the history of the racing car.

A youthful Raymond Mays at the wheel of his Bugatti Brescia 'Cordon Rouge' in 1922. (The Author's Collection)

Bugatti Type 35, 35B, 35C and 35T

The first Bugatti that could be considered pure Grand Prix, and was actually called the Grand Prix model, was the Type 35. It made its debut at the French

Grand Prix of 1924, and though it was not an instant success (few Bugattis were), it developed into the personification of Grand Prix Bugatti and the one that everyone wants, or copies. Up to this point Bugatti design still had a distinct 'Edwardian' air about it, but the Type 35 Grand Prix was to change all that. Although it was typical of the vintage years of Grand Prix racing, it was not a 'state-of-the-art' design when it first appeared, having only one overhead camshaft and no supercharger, but it did boast three valves per cylinder and it was a straight-eight, the 60 × 88 mm cylinders giving 1991 cc to comply with the Grand Prix Formula.

The chassis was finely designed, tapering from each end to maximum beam-strength in the centre, the front axle was circular in section and the bodywork was aesthetically very satisfying, even though it was of two-seater width. The special Grand Prix wheels, cast in aluminium with integral brake drums, were to make the Grand Prix Bugatti stand out among lesser cars.

Within two years the Grand Prix Bugattis were finding plenty of customers, as they were sold 'ready to race,' and it is probable that every one built was used in some form of motoring competition. The basic design remained unchanged right through to 1931, though there were many variations on the theme. A supercharger was added, which also added a C to the Type number (C for *compressor*). When the stroke was increased to 100 mm to give 2262 cc, the car became known as Type 35B. This last model was the epitome of the series, known affectionately as the 'Blown two-three Bugatti'. A less highly tuned version, more suited to sports car racing, was the 35T and there was a 1½-litre version known as the Type 39 or 39A when fitted with a supercharger. The smaller capacity was achieved by a variety of configurations, but usually using a short-throw crankshaft of only 66 mm throw, retaining the standard 60 mm bore. All these variations on the Type 35 theme had full roller-bearing crank shaft and rods, and were essentially competition cars. Including the 1½-litre cars, a total of 210 were built, 90 with superchargers.

As a sort of 'boy-racer' a cooking version of the Type 35 was marketed, using a touring 2-litre engine with plain big end bearings and only three main-bearings.

The Bugatti Type 35C 2-litre car of George Eyston in the paddock at Brooklands in 1927.
(The Geoffrey Goddard Collection)

This was the 35A known as the *Course Imitation* or *Tecla*, but apart from wire-spoke wheels in place of cast alloy and coil ignition replacing the magneto, the external differences were minimal. The engine was however limited to 4000 rpm, whereas the full roller-bearing engines could run to 5500 rpm, so it was essential not to get the two models muddled up! A total of 130 of these imitation Grand Prix Bugattis were built, but as all the components of the whole Type 35 series had a consistency of design, it is probable that many 35A cars were rebuilt as 35 or 35C and this is still happening today.

Although a very large proportion of the output of Type 35 Bugattis and the variations, have survived, there are not enough to go round, as everyone wants a Grand Prix Bugatti. Consequently the old-car market-place has seen prices rise to ridiculous heights, and a very solid industry has grown up manufacturing new components for these desirable cars. Naturally this has led to the business of building complete cars from newly made spares and there are now nearly as many 'Facsimiles' as there are genuine cars. The dividing line between what is a genuine Grand Prix Bugatti, made in Molsheim, and a 'Facsimile' made in England, France, America, Belgium, Australia or Germany is very fine and the honesty of the builder/owner/vendor is paramount in the Bugatti world. Such is the proliferation of newly made parts, from chassis frames to complete engines, that the Bugatti fancier can more or less specify the model he wants before it is assembled. Many of the genuine cars have a slight edge in the desirability stakes as they can be traced to have had an interesting competition career, even to winning Grand Prix races, but if you are only interested in the fun of driving a Grand Prix Bugatti you would not be disappointed with a 'Facsimile', as some of them are better than new.

Bugatti Type 37 and 37A

So popular was the straight-eight Grand Prix Bugatti as a competition car and a sports car, that Bugatti put into production a simpler and cheaper version with a 4-cylinder engine. This was virtually half of the Grand Prix engine, but with plain big end bearings and a bore of 69 mm to give 1496 cc with the 100 mm stroke.

The 4-cylinder 1½-litre Bugatti Type 37. (The Author)

The Bugatti Type 37A engine with Roots-type supercharger. (The Author)

Although the car was marketed in standard trim with wire-spoke wheels, it was a simple matter to convert to the alloy wheels, though an expensive extravagance on a 1½-litre car. The Type 37 Grand Prix 4-cylinder was a very worthy little car and well able to compete in races and speed trials, and because of its keen following in the sporting world the supercharged Type 37A was offered, and a well-tuned 37A was faster than a mediocre straight-eight Grand Prix Bugatti.

A total of 290 cars were built, 67 of them supercharged, though many of the unblown ones were converted, for the whole range of Grand Prix Bugattis was like a huge Meccano set and you could more or less build what you felt you wanted. A large proportion of the 4-cylinder Grand Prix cars have survived, though many have been used to make eight-cylinder Type 35 variants, the chassis, body and bulkheads being essentially the same on all Grand Prix models. Gearbox, clutch, front and rear axles, and brake actuation are interchangeable between Type 37 and Type 35.

History

In effect the Type 37 and Type 37A cars were the 'poor man's Grand Prix car.' They did not have the excitement and charisma of the 2-litre and 2.3-litre 8-cylinder cars, but were first-class little cars, and not at all imitation as might be thought. 'Facsimiles' have been built, but many genuine cars have been cannibalized to make more exciting cars.

Bugatti Type 51 and 51A

In Grand Prix racing Ettore Bugatti always seemed to lag behind the accepted standards, only taking to supercharging after everyone else was well developed, and eschewing hydraulic brakes almost to the end of his Grand Prix career. Simi-

larly he stuck to his single overhead camshaft and three valves per cylinder layout long after every well-known engine designer was using two-valves in a hemispherical combustion chamber with two overhead camshafts. However, he finally went the 'twin-cam' route in 1931 and created the Type 51 Bugatti Grand Prix model, with a 1½-litre version known as the 51A.

The whole design of the car was identical to the Type 35 Grand Prix series, differing outwardly only in details. The hole in the bonnet on the right-hand side for the supercharger pressure release valve outlet was lower, the twin-cam top end necessitating a shorter inlet manifold from the supercharger mounted alongside the crankcase. Just as the Type 35B was known as 'the Blown two-three' the Type 51 was known as 'The double-wipe two-three'. The Type 51A used a 66 mm stroke crankshaft giving 1493 cc and a few cars were built with 88 mm stroke, giving 1991 cc and known as the 51C. These twin-cam cars were in production from 1931 to 1935 and a total of 40 were built, a large proportion of them having survived, as they were competitive in Club events right up to 1939. In Grand Prix racing they were a fair match for the Alfa Romeo and Maserati opposition in their early years, but were superseded in 1934 by the Type 59.

Even today a well-tuned Type 51 Bugatti has a straight-line performance bordering on the Super Car category, and of all the Bugatti racing engines the 'twin-cam' is probably the best, and certainly the most exciting to look at and listen to.

With the instant changeability of parts between various Grand Prix models, many of the Type 51 cars have lost their identity over the years, and since the 'cult' of Bugatti has expanded in recent years there has been a lot of controversy over what is a genuine Type 51 and what is not. This is not only because new ones are being made, but over the years many of them have been taken apart, bits lost or transferred, and those people trying to reconstruct genuine cars have a lot of problems, especially when they find another Type 51 with the same engine or chassis number! This whole business of genuine, fake or muddled identities of Grand Prix Bugattis is far too complex for this book to deal with. The Bugatti Owners Club historians are confused, and they specialize in the cars. The safest outlook is that all Grand Prix Bugattis are suspect until proved genuine.

Bugatti Type 59

This was Ettore Bugatti's last serious attempt at a Grand Prix car, with a works team intended to challenge Alfa Romeo, Maserati and the new German teams of Mercedes-Benz and Auto Union in 1934. These cars, which embodied many new ideas that broke away from the traditional Grand Prix Bugatti, made their debut at the Spanish Grand Prix in 1933. For the new Grand Prix Formula in 1934, which stipulated a maximum weight of 750 kilograms, without tyres, water and oil, the Type 59 was very marginal and a certain amount of craft had to be exercised at scrutineering when the cars were weighed. At the French Grand Prix the car that René Dreyfus drove only just scraped in, scaling 749.5 kg. By the new standards being set by the German teams, the Type 59 Bugatti was already obsolete, both as regards power output from its supercharged straight-eight engine, road-holding with its stiff leaf-springs on rigid axles, and braking, the operation still being by cables when everyone else had gone over to hydraulic operation. Against the Germans and the Scuderia Ferrari Alfa Romeos the Type 59 cars were 'no-hopers' but they did manage a few results in lesser events.

In 1935 four of the six works cars were offered for sale in the latest form, with 3.3-litre engines, and all four were sold to Great Britain. They were bought by Lord Howe, C. E. C. Martin, A. H. L. Eccles and Noel Rees, the last-named being the entrant and sponsor of the Hon. Brian Lewis. Even in British National racing the Type 59 cars were not a huge success and could not really match the Tipo B *monoposto* Alfa Romeos that had also been unloaded on the British, having become obsolete in Grand Prix racing. Apart from not being able to win, the Type 59 was proving rather fragile and unreliable and both Brian Lewis and Charlie Martin soon gave up the unequal battle.

While the British were struggling on their home ground the works team of Wimille and Benoist continued to take part in Grand Prix events with two more Type 59 cars during 1935, but the end was in sight for Bugatti, and for the French, as far as Grand Prix racing was concerned. By 1936 France had opted out of Grand Prix racing, many of her established events becoming sports car races, and Bugatti supported the move and converted one of the Type 59 cars into a sports car, with just sufficient road equipment to satisfy the scrutineers.

By 1936 the Noel Rees car had been sold to the USA, Martin had sold his to the Duke of Grafton, Lord Howe had actually achieved a lap of the Brooklands track at 138.34 mph, to become the fourth fastest car to lap the Surrey track, and Lindsay Eccles had been forced to give up motor racing. The Duke of Grafton crashed in his first race with the Martin car and killed himself, and Arthur Baron bought the wreckage and rebuilt it, fitting an E.N.V. pre-selector gearbox with a view to using the car for sprints and hill-climbs. In 1937 Howe sold his car to South Africa, Jack Lemon-Burton bought the Eccles car and C. I. Craig bought the Lewis car back from America. Up to the outbreak of war the three cars in England were quite active at club level. Craig rebuilt his car in a rather garish manner, painting it black and white with masses of chromium plate, and competed in sprint events; Arthur Baron was active in similar events with his car, in a more sober dark blue, and Lemon-Burton raced his on the Brooklands Campbell Circuit and Mountain Circuit, enlarging the engine to 3.8 litres and fitting Lockheed hydraulic brakes.

During the war years all three cars changed hands, though naturally they were never used, but once competition motoring returned in 1946 they were active once more. George Abecassis bought the Baron car, and used it in any events that were

'Doc' Taylor drives up to the start line at Prescott with his Type 59 Bugatti.
(Guy Griffiths)

organized, while the other two cars were converted into road-going sports cars, and were used in competitions as Super Sports Cars, which indeed they were. Both of them were converted by Rodney Clarke and Louis Giron, under the cloak of Continental Cars Ltd, which was specializing in Bugattis. The Lewis/Craig car was returned to a more normal French blue and registered LPG 211, while the Eccles/Lemon-Burton car, still with 3.8-litre engine and hydraulic brakes, was registered DBL 241.

In 1949 Kenneth Bear had acquired the Martin/Baron car from Abecassis and crashed during practice for the Jersey Road Race and was killed, the second time this car had killed its driver. For a long while the wreckage lay fallow, but eventually it was rebuilt by Stafford-East and has recently been seen 'on demonstration'. LPG 211 eventually went to America, where it was photographed more than it was driven, and DBL 241 stayed in the UK and was used as a road car. This last car also ended up in an American collection, after undergoing a complete rebuild before it left England, to its 1935 state, with the engine reduced back to 3.3 litres, the return of cable brakes and devoid of road equipment. Previous to this the American owner of LPG 211 had had it rebuilt and highly polished, and it too reverted to pure Grand Prix form, no longer road-usable.

In 1964 the Lord Howe car was brought back from South Africa, where it had led a fairly sheltered life, and it returned to England to enter the world of VSCC activity and Historic racing. In 1986 it made a reappearance in Vintage racing, rebuilt ten years after it had been crashed, and in the hands of its appreciative owner Neil Corner, showed that though it may have been near-obsolete when it was conceived, it was undoubtedly the fastest Grand Prix Bugatti of them all.

The Bugatti Owners Club seem undecided as to exactly how many Type 59 cars were built by the factory, putting the number at 'six or seven'. Certainly there were six as 1935 racing history shows, and five of them still exist. The four 'English' ones, as chronicled above, and the factory car that was converted into a sports car and in use up to the middle of 1939, for this car is now in the Schlumpf Museum in Mulhouse. In 1938 the Bugatti factory produced a rather old-fashioned car for the new 3-litre Grand Prix Formula that was a pure single-seater, or *monoplace*, with the driver sitting centrally, and much of this car followed the Type 59 design and components. A special hill-climb single-seater with a 4.7-litre engine made sporadic appearances between 1935 and 1939, and again after the war. Both of these single-seaters used the radially-spoked wire-wheels with integral brake drums that were a feature of the Type 59. In the Type 59 context the factory built a pure sports car, based on the Type 59 layout, for the King of Belgium, their second 1935 works Type 59, with a sports engine and gearbox, and this car is still alive and well and often mistakenly regarded as a Type 59.

History

Built by the Bugatti factory for their works team for the 1934–37 Grand Prix Formula of 750 kilograms. Six cars built, of which four raced in England in 1935. All four have remained in existence with documented and detailed history right through to the present day. Two are in American collections, two remain in England in private hands. Of the two factory team cars raced in 1935 one was converted into a sports/racing car in 1936 and today is in the Schlumpf Museum, the second was converted into a road-going sports car, and lives in Belgium. The 1938 *monoplace* 3-litre version that was in effect a Type 59 went to America when the Bugatti firm closed down, and the one-off hill-climb car, with 4.7-litre engine, is in the Schlumpf Museum.

Type 59

Chassis No. 59121	Factory team car. Purchased by Charlie Martin in 1935. Bought by Duke of Grafton and crashed in 1936. Rebuilt by Arthur Baron. Raced in 1946 by George Abecassis, then Kenneth Bear. Crashed in Jersey 1949. Rebuilt and owned by Stafford-East. 'Genuine'.
Chassis No. 59122	Factory team car. Bought by Lindsay Eccles in 1935. Sold to Jack Lemon-Burton, who fitted special crankshaft to give 3.8-litre capacity. Fitted hydraulic brakes. Made into a road-going sports car after the war, registered DBL 241. Owned by Carr, Roberts and de Ferranti. Sold to USA in 1986. 'Genuine'.
Chassis No. 59123	Factory team car. Bought by Lord Howe in 1935. Lapped Brooklands at 138.34 mph. Sold to South Africa. Returned to UK in 1964. Still active in VSCC racing with present owner Neil Corner. 'Genuine'.
Chassis No. 59124	Factory team car. Bought by Noel Rees for Hon. Brian Lewis to race in 1935. Sold to USA in 1936. Returned to UK in 1937 and 'tarted up' by Craig in 1938, painted black and white. After war converted into sports car and registered LPG 211. Went to USA and stayed there. Still in American collection. 'Genuine'.

Bugatti Monoplace

This one-off car built by the Bugatti factory was something of an enigma, for it has never been very clear as to why it was built. If it had been intended for the 1934–37 Grand Prix Formula it was too heavy, and if the idea had been Formule Libre

Jean-Pierre Wimille with the 1939 Bugatti 4.7-litre Monoplace *in the first post-war race held in the Bois de Boulogne in 1945.* (The Geoffrey Goddard Collection)

events, for which Ferrari built the *Bi-motore* Alfa Romeo, it did not appear in them. It was loosely based on the Type 59, using the same wheels and brakes, but the engine was a 4.7-litre version of the Type 50 engine used in the Formule Libre Type 54 Grand Prix car. It was used in French hill-climbs and in 1939 the factory sent it to the Bugatti Owners Club Prescott hill-climb, with Jean-Pierre Wimille as the driver and Jean Bugatti in attendance. It was patently too big for the twisty Gloucestershire hill and the best that Wimille could do was to finish third, behind a 2-litre E.R.A. and 2-litre Alta. Using twin rear wheels, to aid traction and cope with the power of the big straight-eight supercharged engine, the car was too wide to use the rough return road from the top of the hill, and proceedings had to be held up after each run to allow this impressive car to return to the paddock by way of the hill itself. This was a bonus for spectators, who had a chance to see the car again as it descended leisurely down the hill.

After the war the factory produced the car for the first race meeting in Europe, held in the Bois de Boulogne in Paris in September 1945. Driven by Wimille it had no difficulty in winning the main event, which encouraged Bugatti enthusiasts to think that the Bugatti factory was going to regain its former glory, but this was not to be. When the Molsheim factory closed down the big *Monoplace* was acquired by the Schlumpf brothers, and today this impressive Bugatti factory special resides in the museum in Mulhouse.

Bugatti Type 73C

It is often thought that the Bugatti firm declined after the death of Ettore Bugatti in 1947, but it is much more likely that the decline set in in 1939, when his brilliant son Jean was killed in a road accident. By the time of Ettore's death some rather unimaginative production cars were being planned and a series of new racing cars had begun, but not finished. These were the Type 73C and it is difficult to see how they were going to fit into the post-war racing scene. The engine was a 4-cylinder

The Type 73C Bugatti in the Donington Collection. The body is modern and represents what its restorers consider that it would have looked like. (The Geoffrey Goddard Collection)

with twin overhead camshafts, but bearing no resemblance to the pre-war twin-cams, and with a tiny little supercharger mounted on the front of the crankshaft. The engine was installed in a 'vintage'-style channel-section chassis with rigid-axle suspension front and rear, the whole affair so dated in comparison with the then current Alfa Romeo and Maserati Grand Prix cars that it was difficult to take it seriously. Although 1947 is always given as the base-line for the Type 73C, had it been 1937 it would have been out of date, and 1927 would have been nearer the mark.

One car, in bare chassis form, finished up in the Schlumpf collection, another was acquired by the Donington Collection and a third was acquired by English Bugatti enthusiasts who actually completed it and had it running at VSCC meetings before selling it to a Japanese collector. The Donington car was given a body-work reminiscent of the 1938 Grand Prix 3-litre Bugatti, and looks acceptable as a pre-war design. A fourth incomplete set of parts also exist.

Over the years the Bugatti factory did some strange things, but the 73C was one of the strangest.

Bugatti Type 251

The last Grand Prix Bugatti to emanate from the Molsheim factory was a monumental folly that was not only a total failure, but was bizarre in the extreme and rather sad to see for anyone who had known Bugatti in the heyday. The Type 251 was built to the 2½-litre unsupercharged Grand Prix Formula of 1954–60. Two cars were built and made their appearance at the French Grand Prix at Reims in 1956, with Maurice Trintignant as the nominated driver. Many people viewed this

The rear-engined Bugatti Type 251 at Reims in 1956. This car was the second of the type to be built. (LAT)

factory entry as the great return of a famous name, but it was not to be; it turned out to be the death of a famous name.

The car had been designed by Gioacchino Colombo, the Italian who had been with Alfa Romeo and Ferrari, and was ingenious if nothing else. It was ahead of its time in having the engine mounted behind the driver, but the large straight-eight Bugatti engine was mounted *transversely* ahead of the rear axle assembly. Suspension was a complicated arrangement of links, bell-cranks and levers operating remotely mounted coil spring units and the car was very short and very fat. Engineering direction of the 251 was by Pierre Marco and the firm was being directed by Ettore's younger son Roland Bugatti.

Apart from lacking in power, relative to its contemporaries, the handling was not brilliant, and though Trintignant drove both cars during practice, the earlier prototype was used for the race and lasted only a few laps. The two cars were returned to Molsheim and never seen again until the Schlumpf brothers acquired them, and they now sit in the museum at Mulhouse.

Acknowledgements to Bugatti Owners Club.

C.T.A. Arsenal

The French seem to have a penchant for making technical disasters under the guise of Grand Prix cars. They are invariably heralded as 'national saviours against the foreign hordes', but seldom have they succeeded. Indeed, many of them have barely raced, and few have gone out in a blaze of patriotic glory.

One such was the C.T.A. Arsenal, an ambitious project launched by the Centre d'Études Techniques de l'Automobile et du Cycle, a Government-backed research centre. C.T.A. was an abbreviation of the long-winded official name, and Arsenal came from the fact that much of the engineering was carried out in the State Arsenal. This was in 1946, during the years of recovery from the war, and cost did not seem to enter into the equation. In those days you did not buy your ready-made Grand Prix engine from a specialist firm, nor did you assemble a chassis from

Raymond Sommer in practice for the 1947 French Grand Prix at Lyon with the C.T.A. Arsenal. (Motor)

specialist components, everything had to be designed and manufactured from scratch.

This ambitious Grand Prix car was a 1½-litre V-8 with two-stage supercharging, four overhead camshafts, dual ignition and a claimed 266 bhp at 7500 rpm. It was mounted in a quite advanced chassis with all wheels independently sprung and was clothed with a very sleek bodywork contemporary to the times. Within a year the first car was running on test, and it was entered in the 1947 French Grand Prix at Lyon. After a troubled practice session it appeared on the starting grid only to break a drive-shaft when the driver let the clutch in.

The following year a second car was completed and they appeared for practice for the French Grand Prix, this time at Reims. They were far from ready to race and after practice were withdrawn, never to be seen in action again. In later years they were sold to the Talbot-Lago firm, which did nothing with them, and when Talbot closed down they went into limbo in Paris. Eventually one of them surfaced in a French museum, looking very sad and down at heel, obviously having been neglected for many years. It still resides in France in a museum collection, but it is unlikely that it will ever be resuscitated and made to perform, the memory of this expensive failure still being an embarrassment to many French racing enthusiasts.

History

Two cars manufactured in the French State Arsenal to the design of Albert Lory for the *Centre d'Études Techniques de l'Automobile et du Cycle*. The first one appeared at the French Grand Prix of 1947, and this and a second one practised for the French Grand Prix in 1948. Not seen running in public again, though one has been on display in a museum.

Cisitalia D46 and Type 360

The Cisitalia firm was formed immediately after the war in 1946 by Piero Taruffi and Piero Dusio to manufacture small racing and sports cars. Their factory was in Turin, so it was no surprise to find that their cars were based on Fiat components.

The pretty little D46 model was a single-seater built on a tubular space-frame, using Fiat-inspired independent front suspension and an 1100 cc Fiat engine and gearbox. Sufficient of these cars were built to allow 'one-make' races'and a travelling circus was envisaged in which Grand Prix drivers would race against each other in these little cars before the serious business of the day. This was an idea that was re-born by B.M.W. with their M1 coupés in recent times in their Pro-car Series. The Cisitalia D46 idea did not get far, as after one or two events the novelty wore off, just as it did in later years with the M1 B.M.W. coupés.

Various amateur drivers bought the little Cisitalias for national club events and mountain hill-climbs, and a handful have survived, mostly in Italian and Swiss collections and museums.

The racing driver Harry Schell, the original 'American in Paris', brought one to a Shelsley Walsh meeting in the late 1940s, and Frank Kennington drove it in a race at Goodwood, but customs and excise problems saw it return to its native Italy.

Rather than develop the D46 as a serious 'voiturette' and eventual Formula 2 and Formula 1 design, as Amédée Gordini did with his similar cars in France, Dusio became ambitious and commissioned a truly exotic Grand Prix car from the Porsche Design Studio, run by Ferry Porsche while his illustrious father was still interned by the French authorities after the war. This Grand Prix car also had a tubular space-frame, but was years ahead of its time and far too complex and costly for Cisitalia to support. The engine was a horizontally opposed 12-cylinder, with four camshafts and two superchargers. It was mounted in the centre of the chassis, behind the driver, and drove to a 5-speed all-synchromesh gearbox and the power

A Cisitalia D46 in the paddock at Goodwood in August, 1949. It was driven by Frank Kennington. (Guy Griffiths)

The Cisitalia 360 seen minus its bodywork.

was then transmitted to all four wheels, the drive to the front wheels being optional and controlled by a lever on the steering column.

One car was completed, but never raced, and there was a second set of parts for a further car. However, this was all too much for Dusio and Cisitalia collapsed, Dusio disappearing off to Argentina and taking the completed Grand Prix car with him. Out there he formed a new company called Autoar and actually got the car running, but that was it and the whole project faded into obscurity.

Many years later the Porsche factory acquired the car, and back in Stuttgart it was rebuilt and put into full working order and today holds a place of honour in the Porsche Museum in Zuffenhausen.

The collection of parts for the second car was gathered up and eventually Tom

Wheatcroft acquired them for his Donington Collection. He assembled the car as far as was possible and had a body built identical to the complete car in the Porsche museum. It sits on display as one of the most exciting 'might-have-beens' of the Grand Prix world.

History

Designed as Project 360 by Ferry Porsche and his design team for the Cisitalia firm of Turin in 1947. Completed but never raced in Europe. Taken to Argentina by Piero Dusio when his Cisitalia firm was liquidated. Practised briefly for the 1953 Buenos Aires Grand Prix, but not raced. Returned to the Porsche factory in 1959, rebuilt and put on display in the factory museum. Second car never completed. Parts acquired by the Donington Collection and partially assembled as a show exhibit.

Cognac Special

This special or 'Bitza' has been around so long that it has to be historic, even though its origins are obscure. The earliest traceable reference to it was in a Speed Trial in the 1930s, when it was down in the programme as the Cognac Special of 1991 cc capacity and driven by Mr S. A. Cohen. That in itself meant little, but knowing the car had been concocted pre-war, using a very early G.N. chassis powered by an A.C. 6-cylinder engine of 1991 cc, it is not difficult to see where the name Cognac came from CO-Cohen, GN-chassis, AC-engine.

Like many specials of that period it had little value and after the war languished about the place until bought by Ron Footitt, who still owns it some 35 or more years later. The chassis frame was traced to being a G.N. of 1921 and the A.C. Six engine was identified at 1925, and what better combination of bits to build a 'Bitza'

Ron Footitt with the Cognac Special at Shelsley Walsh in August, 1949. (Guy Griffiths)

in about 1935. Since Ron Footitt acquired it he has used it in every form of vintage competition imaginable, even to fitting it with mudguards and silencer and competing in road events. It has always been a strong competitor in speed trials and hill-climbs, and in relatively short Historic races at circuits such as Oulton Park, Silverstone and Cadwell Park.

If ever there was a classic case of the executioner's original axe, the Cognac must be it, for with the passage of time and the vast amount of competition work it has done almost everything on the car has been worn out or broken. With six new heads and four new handles, it is still the original axe! One thing that Ron Footitt has retained throughout its long life is the spirit of the original Cognac Special. It has never been fitted with a rigid tubular chassis, nor independent front suspension nor a pre-selector gearbox, nor has it ever had a 'modernized' body shape. Naturally development work has gone on in the engine department and in the brakes and shock-absorbers and it is now so fast that it is a continual embarrassment to more sophisticated cars with high pedigrees. The Cognac has no pedigree; it doesn't need one, it is an honest special. 'Continuous.'

Connaught

Connaught Engineering made single-seater racing cars for Formula 2 and Formula 1 between the years 1949 and 1956. The original intention had been to make the cars strictly for sale, but development-through-racing was part of the philosophy of Rodney Clarke and Mike Oliver, the two men behind the project, so they ran a factory team alongside their customers. The first prototype car appeared during the 1950 season and was to the current Formula 2 rules, with unsupercharged engine. This was the start of the A-series, of which nine were eventually built.

The chassis frame consisted of two large-diameter tubular members, suitably cross-braced and incorporating the oil tank in the front cross-member, which was also the structure for carrying the wishbone pivots of the front suspension. Similar wishbones were used at the rear and the suspension medium was torsion bars. The wheelbase was 7 ft 6 in and into this chassis was installed a 1767 cc Lea-Francis racing engine coupled to an Armstrong Siddeley pre-selector gearbox. Pannier fuel tanks were mounted on each side of the chassis and one of the concepts of Connaught design was self-evident: to keep all the weight masses within the wheelbase in the interests of a low polar moment of inertia and good, neutral handling.

Financial benefactor to Connaught Engineering was Kenneth McAlpine, and he raced the prototype A-series car throughout 1951, during which time the independent rear suspension gave way to a de Dion layout, and the wheelbase was reduced to 7 ft 1 in. Connaught did their own development work on the Lea-Francis engine, enlarging it to 2 litres and improving the power output dramatically. During this development year it had been intended to build A2, but somehow this never got done and A1 remained the 'works' car.

In 1952 four cars were built, and raced by Ken Downing. Philip Fotheringham-Parker, Eric Thompson and Leslie Marr in company with McAlpine in A1. At the end of the season A7 was built and exhibited at the London Motor Show.

In 1953 another new A-series was built and taken into the works team, alongside A1 and A7, this being A8, while the customer-cars continued to race with new owners in some cases. Principal developments to the works cars were the use of Hilborn-Travers fuel injection, nitro-methane laced fuel and adjustable anti-roll bars for the rear suspension. Two more cars were built during 1953, AL9 and AL10, the 'L' signifying long wheelbase, as this was extended to 7 ft 6 in, the wheelbase of the prototype in original form. The first of these was sold to John Lyon and the second one joined the works team. A8 left the team and was sold to Guy Jason-Henry.

At all times the A-series Connaught was a good car to drive, invariably the fastest British Formula 2 car, but unable to compete against Ferrari and Maserati simply through a lack of power, the Connaught-developed Lea-Francis engine never giving more than 140 bhp. On handling and road-holding it was way ahead of the opposition and always looked very undramatic, a classic example of 'cornering-on-rails'. Even today, in Historic racing, an A-type Connaught corners fast and steady, making its contemporaries look very old-fashioned. Without doubt the Connaughts were well designed and well made, for those that are still very active are almost embarrassingly original, none having had to be 'resurrected' from a rusty old heap of bits, like some supposedly famous Historic cars.

In 1954 the International Formula 2 was dropped and replaced by a new Formula 1, so while the A-series cars continued to race in British club events, Connaught set about building their B-series cars to the new Formula, which allowed for 2½-litre engines.

The A-series Connaught driven by Kenneth McAlpine at the 1952 International Trophy at Silverstone. (Guy Griffiths)

In 1953 Connaught raced the A-series with Hilborn-Travers fuel injection. This is Roy Salvadori in the British Grand Prix at Silverstone. (T. C. March)

A completely new car was designed, using much of the knowledge gained with the A-series cars. Coil spring/damper units were used with double-wishbone front suspension, but torsion bars were retained for the de Dion layout at the rear. The large-diameter tubular frame was braced and stiffened by a lighter tubular super-structure. Dunlop alloy wheels and disc brakes were used, and in conjunction with Geoffrey Taylor the firm developed a 2½-litre version of his 4-cylinder Alta engine, running on Weber carburettors. The engine was still carried fairly far forward in the chassis, but the pre-selector gearbox was moved back and coupled to the chassis-mounted final drive unit.

It was late in 1954 before the new car was completed and it startled the racing world, as it had a full-width streamlined body which covered all the wheels, with a large fairing behind the cockpit running into a high tail fin. This was B1, and it became the works car for 1955, when the B-type began racing. B2 was to the same specification, and went to McAlpine, while B3, also a 'streamliner,' was sold to

Tony Rolt at the wheel of Rob Walker's unstreamlined B-series Connaught in the 1955 British Grand Prix at Aintree. (T. C. March)

The final development of the B-series raced by the works was the 'dart-shaped' or 'toothpaste-tube' car seen here with Stuart Lewis-Evans at the wheel in the 1957 Monaco Grand Prix. This was the team's last race and Lewis-Evans finished fourth. Note the short nose fitted specially for Monaco. (LAT)

Leslie Marr. The next customer, Rob Walker, did not want the all-enveloping streamlined body, so B4 was built with a conventional single-seater open-wheel bodywork.

During the season B1 was crashed badly at Aintree and Connaught realized the impracticability of the expensive all-enveloping streamlined bodywork and rebuilt the car with orthodox bodywork, like B4.

The technical progress in the new Formula 1 was very rapid; as big firms joined in, small firms were falling by the wayside and Connaught found it hard to keep up. At the end of the 1955 season the works team won the Syracuse Grand Prix, beating the Maserati team, using the rebuilt B1 with Tony Brooks at the wheel, so that all future B series cars became known as the Syracuse model. Although B2 was kept as a 'streamliner' for a time, it was eventually rebodied in open-wheel form.

By 1956 it was clear that private owners had little hope of competing in Grand Prix events, and Connaught concentrated on the works team with B5, B6 and B7 all to 'Syracuse' specification, although an Italian private owner had bought B7 and raced it along with the works drivers in a couple of events.

Although the works team ran strongly throughout 1956, no further B-series cars were built and for 1957 the team bought B3 back from Leslie Marr and used it as a 'guinea-pig' car. It had briefly had a Jaguar 3.4-litre engine installed for participation in Tasman racing in New Zealand, but was rebuilt with an Alta-Connaught 2½-litre engine and a totally new bodywork. This was of the open-wheel type but explored interesting aerodynamic theories based on the wedge principle, the highest point being at the end of tail. At the works it was dubbed 'Moby Dick' for obvious reasons, while the outside world dubbed it the 'toothpaste tube'.

The factory team began 1957 with all the B-series cars on their strength with the sole exception of B4, which was still owned by Rob Walker. The season started on a bad note when they took B1, B2 and B5 to Syracuse for the opening European Grand Prix event and B1 was destroyed in a practice accident. A drive-shaft broke, punctured the fuel tank, and the car was burnt out.

The intention was to make a hand-to-mouth living relying on starting-money to keep things viable, but this depended on there being sufficient races. When some of the European events were cancelled, Connaughts plans were scuppered, and they stopped all activity before they went bankrupt. They had made a couple of appearances with 'Moby Dick' and work was well advanced on a C-series car, using a new and lighter chassis frame of small-diameter tubing on the space-frame principle.

Connaught Engineering was closed down and in September 1957 the five cars and equipment were put to auction. All the existing cars had been rebuilt and prepared ready-to-race, and these were B2, B3, B5, B6 and B7. Rob Walker put B4 into the auction, as without the parent firm he could not see much future in racing the car. B1 had been broken up and written off by the firm, and C8 was only partially completed.

Everything was disposed of, except B6 and C8, and was scattered to the four winds of the sporting world, some cars remaining intact, though of little use for serious racing, others being dismantled by well-meaning new owners. The sole C-series car was completed and sold and it actually appeared at a few events, but it was totally outdated by the time this happened. It had a new lease of life when Historic Racing encompassed the B-series and later cars. 'Moby Dick' was eventually resurrected to its original form, with fully streamlined all-enveloping bodywork, and other B-types have appeared infrequently.

All told Connaught built 16 single-seaters which actually raced at the time, plus the partially built C8 and a mock-up of a rear-engined D-series that never saw the light of day. They never built A2 and they scrapped B1.

At the 1957 auction sale the chassis frame that had been intended for A2, which the factory never built, was sold, and subsequently a Connaught 'Facsimile' was built up on this chassis by a private owner. Also, the damaged chassis frame from the scrapped B1 was unearthed and sold, and in recent years a 'Facsimile' of B1 has been built from some spare parts and some newly made parts.

Cooper-Bristol

When the 2-litre Formula 2 became the major category of racing in 1952, the Cooper Car Company was quick to get on the band-wagon. The Mk 1 Cooper-Bristol had a simple welded sheet steel chassis frame, with suspension front and rear on the principle used on their 500 cc cars, which had a transverse leaf-spring with a lower wishbone on each side, to give a simple form of independent suspension. A 6-cylinder Bristol engine and 4-speed gearbox were mounted in the front, driving through an open propshaft to the E.N.V. differential unit mounted on the rear of the frame. A welded aluminium fuel tank sat on the rear of the chassis and a very basic aluminium body covered the mechanical components. Cast alloy wheels and hydraulic brakes were used and the overall weight was kept low by not making anything too complicated. The low weight was important, as the Bristol engine only gave about 135–140 bhp, and Cooper were hoping to compete against the established firms in Formula 2 who had something like 160 bhp available.

In short races, and on twisty circuits, the Cooper-Bristol was very successful, but the real Grand Prix circuits left it a bit breathless. The 1952 Mk 1 cars were raced by Reg Parnell, Alan Brown, Eric Brandon, Mike Hawthorn, John Barber, André Loens and a number of Scottish drivers who drove for David Murray's Ecurie Ecosse. A one-off Mk 1 was built with a 2-litre E.R.A. engine in it, for use in sprints and hill-climbs.

A Mk 2 appeared in 1953, this having an entirely different chassis frame, but was similar in all other respects. The Mk 2 chassis was a tubular space-frame in general concept, though it depended on tube-stiffness in bending for its rigidity, whereas a true space-frame has all tubes in tension or compression. Rodney Nuckey, Tom Cole, Ken Wharton, Bob Gerard, Bob Chase, Jack Brabham, Horace Gould and Reg Hunt had Mk 2 Cooper-Bristols, while Peter Whitehead, Tony Crook and Stirling Moss had Mk 2 cars with 4-cylinder Alta engines installed. In addition, Stirling Moss had the Ray Martin Special built, using an Alta engine and a Martin frame; as some of the components were from the Cooper works, the car was known as a Cooper-Alta, but it was Cooper in name only.

Both marks of Cooper were very functional and easy to drive, and they established quite a good reputation in minor events, even though they looked unstable when being cornered on the limit, as exemplified by Mike Hawthorn. The Bristol racing version of their production engine was remarkably reliable and could be driven really hard without fear of trouble, whereas the Alta engines were quite the reverse.

In 1954 the International Formula changed to 2½ litres, and Formula 1 became very serious. With no suitable engine available, Cooper withdrew from Formula racing and turned to other categories. There was virtually no further use for the Cooper-Bristols and Cooper-Atlas and they quickly disappeared or changed their character. The Hawthorn car was made into a sports car, as was the Crook car, with the Alta engine replaced by a Bristol. Others went to Australia and continued to race and most of those ended up with 6-cylinder Holden engines in them. Some just disintegrated into their component parts. At best these cars were not very well made, and all that remained of some of them was a heap of rusty and useless bits. When interest in the cars began to grow in Historic circles, many of these rusty old heaps of scrap were retrieved and 're-created'. Some genuinely came from the remains of an original car, others came from bits that 'might' have been on a Formula 2 car, but more likely came from a sports Cooper-Bristol. The result was that

The most famous Cooper-Bristol of them all – Mike Hawthorn with the Bob Chase car in the International Trophy at Silverstone in 1952. (T. C. March)

Ken Wharton with his works-supported, tubular chassis Mk II Cooper-Bristol in the 1953 International Trophy at Silverstone. (T. C. March)

many new Cooper-Bristols came on the Historic scene, for the suspension parts were easy to copy and Bristol engines and gearboxes were easy to come by, and any half-skilled tin-basher could make a new body. The only stumbling block were the alloy Cooper wheels, for the quality of the originals was not very high and 20 years saw corrosion and fatigue setting in, unlike a Connaught alloy wheel, for example, which has resisted the dreaded disease. This has meant that any Cooper-Bristol that races in Historic events has had to use modern alloy wheels. If there is a car on its original 1952–53 wheels, then it is not safe to race. This also applied to various important chassis components such as stub axles and king-posts. Nobody has attempted to resurrect a Cooper-Alta, and even if an Alta engine could be found it would be of more value in an Alta chassis.

No Cooper works records exist of the 1952–53 cars, if indeed any were kept at the time, so that individual car histories are pretty vague and open to doubt. Two cars which are unquestionably 'genuine' are Tony Crook's car, which he had built as a Mk 2 with an Alta engine, and later had it made into a 'quasi'-2-seater sports car, with Bristol engine and gearbox, and apart from a brief period when he sold it to a friend, he has owned it ever since, and still retains it today. The other one is the Martin-Cooper-Alta, which resides in a Scottish museum, very much in its original state. It was such a disaster that nobody attempted to 'improve' it, so it has stayed as it was built.

All the other Coopers, Mk 1 and Mk 2, have varying degrees of original bits in them, some being able to be 'resurrected' by removing the Australian Holden engine and gearbox and finding another Bristol unit, while others are only Cooper-Bristol in conception.

The Mk 1 cars were officially the Type 20, the sports car versions were the Type 22, the Mark 2 Bristol-engined cars were the Type 23, and the Cooper-Altas were the Type 24.

Acknowledgements to Doug Nye and his book *Cooper Cars*, published by Osprey Publishing.

Delage

The firm of Louis Delage was active in racing in the Edwardian era, but did not re-appear in Grand Prix racing until 1923. They then produced a low-slung car, with the driver sitting alongside the transmission shaft, for the 2-litre Grand Prix Formula. The engine was a remarkable V-12 unit, with four overhead camshafts, and it breathed through two carburettors.

In 1925 these cars appeared in supercharged form, with two Roots-type blowers, one to each bank of six cylinders; in that form they were very successful, winning the French Grand Prix and the Spanish Grand Prix. One of these cars survived and was in England in the early 1930s. In 1935 it was heavily modified with the idea of running it in the current 'voiturette' races. This meant reducing the capacity to 1½ litres and an attempt was made to improve the road-holding by fitting independent front suspension on the LMB principle, whereby the axle beam was cut in the middle and the two halves pivoted at the centre on a frame extension to give swing-axle geometry. Springing medium was a transverse leaf spring. Unfortunately the engine blew up rather disasterously while on test, which rather put paid to the project. This car sat around unused for many years until it was resurrected, still with its L.M.B. front suspension, and used in VSCC events. The I.F.S. was discreetly covered with an aluminium apron, and the car now resides in the USA.

Another of the V-12 Delage chassis was used in France to construct the Bequet Special, the Delage engine and gearbox being replaced by a 12-litre V-8 Hispano Suiza aero engine, coupled to a Delage-built 2-speed gearbox. In recent years this exciting car has been resurrected and competes regularly in VCSS racing. The Delage engine and gearbox from this car would appear to be those exhibited in the Biscaretti Museum in Turin for many years.

A few years ago one of the very early unblown V-12-engined cars was found in Santiago in Chile. It had been converted into a road-going two-seater of very dull aspect, and was unrecognizable until the bonnet was opened! In a very sorry state it was rescued by an American enthusiast, and he has had the engine rebuilt in

The V-12 Delage 2-litre with Louis Wagner at the wheel in 1925. (The Geoffrey Goddard Collection)

California, and the chassis restored in England, to make a unique Grand Prix Delage. It is a true 'resurrection'.

When the Grand Prix Formula changed from 2 litres to 1½ litres in 1926, Louis Delage set his design staff to work on an entirely new car, still low and offset, but with a straight-eight engine, supercharged by a single blower at the front of the block. For the first year these new cars were a bit of a failure, the exhaust system on the right making the cockpit so hot that the drivers became exhausted.

For 1927 the inlet and exhaust systems were redesigned, changing places, and making the driving compartment more tolerable. From then on the 8-cylinder Delage 1500 cc became a land mark in Grand Prix design. Everything in this beautiful little engine ran on ball or roller races and the power was transmitted through a 5-speed gearbox to the differential unit, which was offset to the left in the rear axle, allowing the driver to sit very low between the propshaft and the chassis side rail in what was a fairly narrow car.

The works team were entered for four major Grand Prix events in 1927 and they won the lot. In 1928 Louis Delage withdrew his team from racing and sold two of the cars, keeping the other two at the Paris factory.

The two that were sold were imported into England by Malcolm Campbell, and he kept one for his own use and sold the other to W. B. Scott. Both cars were raced very successfully into the 1930s, when Campbell sold his car to Earl Howe and Scott sold his to Capt. Davis; the racing Earl used his in International 'voiturette' races, while the Captain restricted his activities to National events.

Meanwhile, Louis Delage had loaned or sold one car to Louis Chiron, who took it to Indianapolis and finished seventh in the 500-mile race of 1929. The remaining car was sold to Raoul de Rovin, who ran it in the first Monaco Grand Prix in 1929. After the Indianapolis race Chiron passed his car on to Robert Senéchal, who competed in the French Grand Prix with it in 1930 and 1931.

When Earl Howe was racing in the 1932 Italian Grand Prix 'voiturette' race at Monza he crashed badly and the Delage was literally bent double round a tree.

Dick Seaman with the Ramponi-rebuilt straight-eight Delage at a Derby & District Club meeting in 1936 at Donington Park. (The Author's Collection)

The engine and gearbox were salvageable, but the chassis was scrapped. Undeterred, his Lordship visited the Delage factory, and as Senéchal's car was sitting there in good order he bought it to continue his racing programme, keeping the remains of the Campbell car as spares.

In 1935 Howe placed an order for a new E.R.A., so the Delage was for sale and Dick Seaman bought it. He had Giulio Ramponi carry out a vast development programme on it, modernizing it with wider-based front springs, hydraulic brakes, very large fuel tank and a total rebuild of the engine. The resultant car was still very much a 1927 Grand Prix Delage, but soon became known as the Seaman-Delage. 1936 was a veritable *tour de force* for the car in 'voiturette' racing, its real claim to fame being the winning of the small-car races in Pescara, Berne and Donington Park on three successive weekends. It clinched Seaman's entry into the Mercedes-Benz Grand Prix team in 1937, so the Delage was sold to Prince Chula, for Bira to race.

Mindful of the Royal cranium, Chula decided that a 10-year-old chassis frame must have been getting fragile, so he got the Delage factory to make a new one. Carried away with enthusiasm for the project, Delage made a new chassis with his latest front suspension, which was independent by means of a top wishbone arm each side, a transverse lower leaf spring and radius arms to locate the stub axles. In typical Chula fashion, two chassis were made, in order to have a spare in the stores. Also, in order to have mechanical spares, Chula bought the other car that was in England, from Capt. Davis. A 'Chula'-Delage was built up, with a new body, and it appeared in 1938, but Bira did not take to it readily, preferring his E.R.A.s, so it was used very little.

When the war came everything Delage was sold to Reg Parnell, and this included the new car, the spare I.F.S. chassis frame, the two 1927 chassis frames, one original and the other with the Seaman modifications, and all the engines and

The straight-eight Delage 1½-litre engine. This photograph was taken in 1936 after the rebuild by Giulio Ramponi. (The Geoffrey Goddard Collection)

gearboxes, etc. After the war Parnell assembled three cars from the vast array of parts, and individual cars lost their identity. The result was three Delage cars, two with the 1937 I.F.S. chassis frames, and one with the Seaman-modified chassis frame. The fourth chassis frame was not built up into a complete car.

These three Delage 'entities' were used extensively in immediate post-war racing. One of the I.F.S. cars was later fitted with an E.R.A. engine and pre-selector gearbox, and in this E.R.A.-Delage form it is still active in VSCC racing. The second I.F.S. car remained unchanged and now resides in the USA. The 'Seaman' car has been preserved, owned for many years by Rob Walker, but now sold to a French enthusiast. While it is legitimately accepted as being the Seaman-Delage, it is not strictly true, for some of the parts came from the other Delage cars, or the spares pool, and some of the parts that really were on the Seaman car got put on to the others during Parnell's time. However, the modified chassis frame and axles undoubtedly are traceable back to 1936. The chassis of the Capt. Davis car remained unused and unmodified, and was eventually acquired by Alan Burnard, who has painstakingly rebuilt it, and all it needs now is the completion of an engine and 5-speed gearbox to return it to its true 1927 specification.

The fourth of the original team cars, that was last raced by de Rovin, eventually found its way to America and ended up in the Briggs Cunningham Museum, where it was kept in superb condition and in full working order. This is the only 100 per cent 'Genuine' car of the famous 1927 works team, though all the others are satisfactorily 'Authentic'.

Delahaye

Although Delahaye made a number of sports cars which could be used in Grand Prix races in stripped form, they only made one pure single-seater. This was known appropriately enough as the *Monoplace*.

The firm had already developed a 4½-litre V-12 engine, with pushrod-operated overhead valves, which they used in racing/sports cars as well as production cars. Two of the sports cars ran in Grand Prix events in 1938, devoid of all road equipment, and looked as if they could be the basis for a successful Grand Prix single-

The 1938 V-12 Delahaye 4½-litre single-seater Monoplace *with de Dion rear axle.* (Autocar)

seater. The *Monoplace* had an interesting chassis, with independent front suspension and a de Dion rear axle layout, using transverse leaf springs at both ends of the car. The rear hubs incorporated reduction gears to give a low drive line and subsequent low propshaft and low engine mounting.

The engine itself was rather bulky, which meant that the complete car was too large compared to the more serious opposition. In addition no more than 250 bhp could be coaxed from the unsupercharged 4½ litres, and this was not enough to combat the supercharged 3-litre cars of the Grand Prix Formula with their 485 bhp. It made very few appearances before it was put to one side.

After the war it reappeared briefly in some French races, run by a private owner, and it had the de Dion assembly removed and an orthodox rigid axle substituted, mounted on conventional half-elliptic springs. It was still not very competitive and it soon disappeared into a private collection. It still lives in France, but is seldom seen. An interesting car, but not a successful one, it made but one appearance in England, when René Dreyfus drove it in the 1938 Donington Grand Prix.
'Genuine'

Derby-Maserati

This single-seater racing car can only be described as a one-off 'curio', though if you need an example of the word 'unique', this is it. The remarkable thing is that it has remained virtually unchanged since the day it built in 1935. This is probably because it was such an awful car that there was nothing that could be done to make any improvement.

It was built by Douglas Hawkes in his Paris Derby factory for his wife Gwenda to drive in 'voiturette' road races. Hawkes was running the French Derby factory that was hell-bent on front-wheel-drive, in line with Citroën, but lacking the engineering power of that firm. He took a 4-cylinder 1½-litre Maserati racing engine and turned it through 180 degrees and coupled it to a Derby gearbox and front-drive unit and the whole assembly was installed in the narrowest chassis frame he could contrive. The shafts driving the front wheels ran through long swinging arm members like wishbones, pivoted on the chassis frame with a transverse leaf-spring below and coupled to the arms by links. A similar system was used at the rear, but of course with hollow shafts forming the swinging arms. Wheel geometry in the Derby factory seems to have been an unknown subject and the car took up some very odd angles when cornered hard.

Gwenda Hawkes (ex-Stewart) drove the car at the International Trophy race at Brooklands in 1935 and also at Dieppe and in the 'voiturette' race before the Swiss Grand Prix at Berne. It was not a success and lay around at the Derby factory or at Hawkes' workshops at Brooklands, and somehow survived the ravages of war. It reappeared on the Vintage racing scene some 20 years ago, after being resurrected from a rather derelict and neglected state, and finally ended up in the Donington Collection of single-seater racing cars. As a single-seater it must be one of the slimmest ever built, the cockpit uncluttered by the usual clutch and bell-housing, gearbox or propshaft, normally encountered in a conventional front-engined single-seater.
'Genuine'

Douglas Hawkes' front-wheel-drive Derby-Maserati seen at Dieppe in 1935. (The Geoffrey Goddard Collection)

Duesenberg

This one-off project was built by Augie Duesenberg in his factory in Indianapolis, not far from the famous Speedway, and was to the order of Count Carlo Felice Trossi, who was then the President of the Scuderia Ferrari. It was something of a 'special' or 'bitsa', for Augie took one of the 1927 single-seater Duesenberg 1½-litre track cars and installed in it a 4¼-litre straight-eight engine that had been built by Fred 'Skinny' Clemons for an unsuccessful Indianapolis programme. Clemons had copied Harry Miller's engine design to produce his two Indy units, with barrel-crankcase, unitary blocks and heads in cast iron, two overhead camshafts driven by a straight-toothed gear 'tower' at the front. They were big and impressive engines blatantly cribbed from Miller.

Augie Duesenberg helped Clemons to finish off this Indianapolis project, and when the whole affair died in 1933 the 'special' for Trossi and the Scuderia Ferrari was built. It was sent to Italy in August 1933, just in time to have Italian Siata hydraulically controlled friction shock absorbers fitted and to run in the Formule

Jack Duller with the ex-Ferrari 4¼-litre Duesenberg on the banking at Brooklands. (The Geoffrey Goddard Collection)

Libre Monza Grand Prix that was held before the Italian Grand Prix, on the Monza track. It was fast and a bit furious, but retired when a cylinder wall broke.

The Ferrari workshops repaired the engine and in 1934 Whitney Straight borrowed it from Trossi with the idea of running it in the 500-mile race organized by the British Racing Drivers Club on the banked Brooklands track. Straight practised with the car, and it was fast enough to approach the existing lap record, but feeling unwell he withdrew his entry before the race. At the end of the season he ran the car in a Brooklands Outer Circuit race and also made an attempt on the lap record, running on his own. In an heroic drive he was timed to lap at 138.15 mph, fast enough to take the class record but not fast enough for the out-and-out lap record.

Straight then took the car to Montlhéry to attack the World Hour record, but after some practice runs he abandoned the idea. In 1935 Jack Duller bought the car and shipped it back to Brooklands, where it was to stay for the rest of its racing life. Duller raced it regularly on the Brooklands track in short handicap events as well as in the annual 500-mile race, but it did not achieve much in the way of results, and he never managed to lap the track at the same speed that Whitney Straight had achieved. Its best lap in Duller's hands was 132.46 mph, but over the years it covered a great number of laps at over 130 mph and was probably reaching 145 mph down the Railway Straight.

Though not a successful Outer Circuit Brooklands car, the ex-Ferrari Duesenberg was a popular competitor and was also driven by Gwenda Stewart and Dick Seaman. It was remarkably reliable and Duller raced it right through to the last meeting at Brooklands in August 1939, when war stopped play.

After the war, with the banked track gone, Duller sold the car into the second-hand motor trade and the engine was taken out and installed in another special. The rest of the car, complete in all respects, was fitted with a 4-litre Ford-Mercury engine and ran in a few club events, until the well-developed V-8 engine was transferred to an Allard.

Eventually the original engine was acquired from the English special and was put back in the Duesenberg chassis, still in the condition that Duller had raced it in at the last Brooklands meeting. It now resides in the Brooklands Museum within the banked track, where it spent the greater part of its life. A fitting resting place for an old warrior.

Recently, the second of the Clemons 2-seater Indianapolis cars surfaced in a Rumanian museum, having been stored in a factory in that country since pre-war days. It still has its original 'Miller copy' Clemons engine. The other Indianapolis two-seater, from which the engine was removed to build the Trossi car, or Ferrari-Duesenberg, lives in California with a 4-cylinder Offenhauser engine installed. 'Genuine '

E.R.A.

The firm of English Racing Automobiles (E.R.A.) was formed by Raymond Mays and Peter Berthon in 1933, after they had successfully developed a supercharged 6-cylinder Riley for short sprint races and hill-climbs. The first E.R.A. was completed in May 1934, and was, in effect, a single-seater version of the 'White Riley' built around a new chassis frame, suspension and axles, designed by Reid Railton.

Murray Jamieson was involved with the supercharging of the engine and Humphrey Cook supplied the finance. This new design of 'voiturette' caught the imagination of the racing fraternity, even though it suffered numerous design faults and teething troubles during its first season. Four cars were built during 1934, subsequently designated A-types, and in 1935 an improved version was offered for sale, known as the B-type. Altogether 13 B-types were built and three of these were developed into C-types, one of which eventually became the lone D-type.

In 1939 a totally new design came from the Bourne works, this being the E-type, but it had more design faults than the original A-type and the war put a stop to racing before it was really raceworthy. After the war a second E-type was completed and private owners tried unsuccessfully to make them both competitive. In 1952 the last E.R.A. was built by the firm, this being a Bristol-powered Formula 2 car given the designation G-type. It was as big a flop as the E-type had been and the whole project was soon abandoned and the car was sold off. E.R.A. Ltd. turned to non-racing activities in the engineering world.

While Peter Berthon had the support of those two brilliant designers Railton and Jamieson, the E.R.A. made progress and established a good reputation. Once Railton had left and gone to America, and Jamieson was sadly killed in a racing accident, Berthon was lost and one failure followed another. In 1939 Humphrey Cook took everything away from the Mays/Berthon combine at Bourne and tried to run the E-type with a small staff at Donington Park. After the war he established the firm at Dunstable, providing spares and advice to drivers still racing the old A- and B-types. Eventually he sold the firm to Leslie Johnson, but after the dismal showing of the G-type it was the end of E.R.A. as far as the racing world was concerned.

Although there were many failures in the history of the firm, there were also a great many successes, especially in British racing and in International 'voiturette' racing up to 1939. Acceleration was the strong point of the E.R.A. and in addition to establishing numerous records, an E.R.A. could almost guarantee to win a speed trial or hill-climb, even against cars of larger capacity. This attribute was assisted by the fact that the E.R.A. was designed to use a Wilson pre-selector gearbox, which gave instantaneous speed-changes with its epicyclic gear trains and operating band-brakes.

Another outstanding attribute of the early E.R.A.s was reliability and durability, which explains why all but one are still in existence and most of them are still

The first A-type E.R.A. photographed at Bourne in 1934. (The Author's Collection)

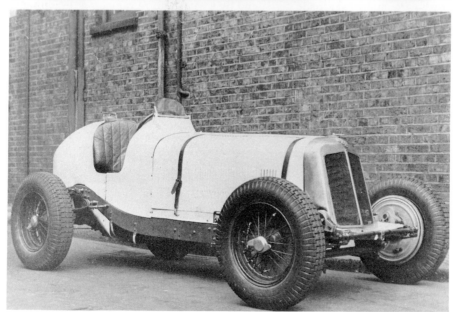

1936 E.R.A. B-type R7B as originally delivered to Arthur Dobson. (The Geoffrey Goddard Collection)

E.R.A. R8C seen at Brooklands in 1938. It started life as a B-type car, but was rebuilt for Earl Howe in 1938. (The Author)

racing in Historic events. The one exception is R3B, which crashed at Deauville in 1936 killing Marcel Lehoux, the Algerian driver. The wreckage was never rebuilt, the damaged parts being scrapped and usable parts put into the second-hand spares store. Four A-types were built, 13 B-types, two E-types and one G-type, making a total of 20 cars to carry the E.R.A. three-ringed badge on the radiator cowl. In recent years two more cars have been constructed from second-hand spare parts and newly made parts, and by a consensus of opinion of present-day owners, both are allowed to carry the E.R.A. badge, and are listed below.

History

The E.R.A. factory was at Bourne in Lincolnshire from 1933 to 1939, where A-types and B-types were built, and B-types were modified into C-types and a D-type. One E-type was built at Bourne before the firm was moved to Donington Park. After the war a second E-type was built at the reconstructed firm at Dunstable on the A5 road, and here the lone G-type was built.

E.R.A. R1A		Factory team car, 1934–35–36. Sold to Norwegian driver E. Björnstad in 1937. Raced by numerous British private owners from 1946 to the present day. Owned by VSCC member and still very active.
	R2A	Factory team car, 1934–35. Sold to Greek driver N. S. ('Nicky') Embiricos in 1936. Fitted with Italian Tecnauto independent front suspension in 1937. Sold to A. C. Pollock in 1938. Raced by him until advent of war. Post-war bought by George Abecassis and raced, sold and bought by long list of owners until the present day. Still very active.
	R3A	Factory team car, 1934–35. First 2-litre engine. Sold to Norman Black 1936 with 1500 cc engine installed, then to Charlie Martin in 1937. Won Avusrennen 'voiturette' race.

Raymond Mays with R4D on the start line at the 1950 Brighton Speed Trials; he set FTD for the fourth time. (Guy Griffiths)

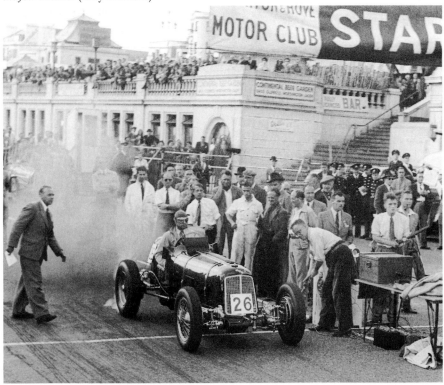

	Sold to Roy Hesketh in South Africa in 1938. Sold to Basil Beall in 1948, raced in Africa until 1952. In 1967 bought back to UK by VSCC member. Still active.
R4A	Built as an 1100 cc version for Pat Fairfield in 1935. First customer for E.R.A. Raced by him 1935–37. Bought by N. G. Wilson after Fairfield's death at Le Mans. Raced until the war. Post-war bought by F. R. Gerard and fitted with 2-litre engine. Sold to Rhodesia and later South Africa in 1956. Returned to UK in 1964 and passed into VSCC member's ownership. Still very active as a 2-litre and with the bodywork alterations made by Gerard.
R1B	First B-type car and second production car. First owner Richard Seaman. Won three major 'voiturette' races in 1935. Sold to G. F. Manby-Colgrave in 1936. Sold to Billy Cotton in 1937 and raced by him until the war. Postwar sold to Cuth Harrison and later passed through the hands of numerous VSCC members. Raced continually and retained in remarkably original condition.
R2B	Bought by HRH Prince Chula of Siam as 21st birthday present for his cousin Prince Birabongse. Raced exclusively by 'Mr B. Bira' from 1935 to 1948. Bira gave the car back to his cousin and it did not race again until 1976. On Chula's death the car passed to his daughter Narissa, and she instigated its rebuilding and limited participation in VSCC Historic events. Car christened 'Romulus' by Prince Chula.

R3B	Built in 1936 as factory team car. Crashed in Deauville race that year and written off. Only E.R.A. to be broken up.
R4B	Factory team car 1935–39. Sold to Raymond Mays in early 1939. Retained and raced by him until 1952. Bought by Ron Flockhart and raced by him 1952–53. Then used by Ken Wharton for hill-climbs. Passed through various hands in the sprint world and progressed into VSCC Historic racing, where it is still very active. For most of its life it has been a 2-litre. Rebuilt as C-type in 1937, with Porsche-designed independent front suspension and hydraulic brakes. Zoller supercharged engine. Rebuilt again as D-type in 1938, using new chassis frame. Post-war had many modifications to suspension, brakes and other mechanical components. Only E.R.A. with steering drag-link on left.
R5B	Built in 1936 for Prince Chula. Raced by Bira in 1936, kept for spares in 1937 and then sold to Tony Rolt. Raced by him 1938–39. Sold to Ian Connell in 1946. Raced continually by various owners. Purchased by Hon. Patrick Lindsay and raced by him in Historic events from 1959 until his death in 1985. Since then raced by his son. Car christened 'Remus' by Prince Chula.
R6B	Built in 1936 for Dr J. D. Benjafield. Sold to D. L. Briault mid-season and raced by him. Sold to Ian Connell in 1937

Leslie Johnson with E-type E.R.A. GP2 in the paddock at Goodwood in April, 1949. Standing behind the car is Eberan von Eberhorst. (Guy Griffiths)

Stirling Moss at the wheel of the offset single-seater G-type E.R.A. in the 1952 British Grand Prix at Silverstone. (T. C. March)

and raced by him 1937–38. Sold to Mrs Hall-Smith for Robin Hanson to race in 1939. Post-war bought by F. R. Gerard and used by him until 1949. Sold into VSCC in 1954 and raced by various owners right through to the present day.

R7B   Built in 1936 for Arthur Dobson. Raced by him until the war. Post-war bought and raced by H. L. Brooke. Then sold to Ken Hutchison, who had a 2-litre engine fitted. Sold in 1952 and not used very much until purchased by D. Gahagan in 1960. Raced continually by him to the present day.

R8B   Built in 1936 for Earl Howe. Raced by him until the war. Rebuilt in 1938 to C-type specification. Post-war bought by Cuth Harrison and rebodied to look 'more modern'. Eventually passed into the world of VSCC racing and later rebuilt to original C-type specification. Still very active.

R9B   Built in 1936 for D. H. Scribbans. Raced by him 1936–37. Sold to R. E. Ansell in 1938 and raced by him until the war, and again post-war by him and others. Sold to Ireland in 1951. Returned to England in 1954 and active in VSCC Historic racing until the present day.

R10B   Built in 1936 for Peter Whitehead. Raced by him and Peter Walker until the war. Successful trip to Australia in 1938. Raced post-war by Whitehead and his half-brother Graham until 1953. Then passed to VSCC members and in continuous use until present day. Still very active.

R11B   Built in 1936 for Reggie Tongue. Raced by him until mid-1938. Sold to Hon. Peter Aitken and raced by him until the war. Post-war passed through various hands, becoming a very successful hill-climb car with Ken Wharton and Michael Christie. Passed to VSCC owners and very active in Historic racing to the present day. One of the fastest E.R.A.s with 2-litre engine. Still very active.

R12B   Factory team car 1936. Rebuilt to C-type specification in 1937. Renumbered R12C. Factory team car in 1937. Sold

	to Prince Chula in 1938. Raced by Bira until the war. Crashed badly in July 1939 and rebuilt to B-type specification on B-type chassis frame. Reverted to R12B. Raced by Bira 1946–47. Sold in 1949 to David Hampshire and David Murray. Raced to 1951. Sold to Rhodesia in 1957. Returned to UK in 1963 and active in VSCC Historic racing to the present day. Still very active and still in 1939 B-type form. Car christened 'Hanuman' by Prince Chula.
R13B	Not built. Number 13 considered unlucky.
R14B	Built as a B-type but with Zoller supercharged C-type engine in 1938 for Johnny Wakefield. Raced by him until the war. Post-war bought by Bob Gerard and raced by him until 1952. Passed into the club world and then into the VSCC world. Bought by Donald Day in 1958 and still owned and raced by him. Spent two years in Far East in 1970–71.
GP1	First E-type car, completed in 1939. Raced by Arthur Dobson for Humphrey Cook. Post-war bought by Peter Whitehead. Bought by Reg Parnell in 1947. Repurchased by Whitehead in 1949 and raced by Peter Walker. Caught fire in Isle of Man race in 1950. The remains were made into a Jaguar-engined sports car. Resurrected as GP1 in recent years.
GP2	Most of the parts were made in 1939, but car was not completed until 1946. Bought by H. L. Brooke. Taken to Indianapolis in 1947 but failed to qualify. Returned to E.R.A. Ltd and raced by new owner of firm, Leslie Johnson. Last raced in 1950. In recent years components retrieved from obscurity and resurrected as GP2 alongside GP1.
G-type	Built by newly owned firm in 1952 using Bristol engine and gearbox. Raced by Stirling Moss. Then sold to Bristol Aeroplane Company Car Division, who used it as the prototype chassis for their Bristol 450 sports/racing coupés.
R12C	This is a reconstruction of a car that was broken up by Prince Chula's White Mouse Team garage in 1939. The original car was R12B, which was converted at the factory into R12C with I.F.S. In 1939 all the usable components were transferred to a B-type chassis frame and the car became R12B. The existing R12C has been constructed from spare parts and newly made parts.
AJM 1	This car has been constructed from spare parts and newly made parts by A. J. (Tony) Merrick, hence the personalized chassis number.

Acknowledgements to *The History of English Racing Automobiles Limited* by David Weguelin, published by White Mouse Editions.

Emeryson Special

An inveterate special builder of the 1930s was 'Pa' Emery, assisted by his son Paul. They ran a garage on the outskirts of south-west London, and while 'Pa' continued with the garage, Paul went to work at the Alta Car & Engineering Company at Tolworth.

After the war father and son built a very successful little racing car on a tubular chassis frame, not unlike a 1939 Alta, with very Alta-like independent rear suspension. At the front they used Singer independent suspension, as used on the larger family Singer saloons in the late thirties, and into this chassis they put an 1100 cc Lagonda Rapier engine. This was a heavy but very strong 4-cylinder unit with twin overhead camshafts and capable of revving freely. The Emerys applied two Marshall superchargers in series, giving a two-stage system of 22 psi, the power passing through an E.N.V. pre-selector gearbox.

This special won one of the first post-war British races, in 1947 at Gransden Lodge aerodrome, and when it was bought by the Irishman Bobby Baird it was taken abroad and run in the French Grand Prix meeting at Lyon in 1947. With 'Voiturette' racing being confined to 2-litre cars without superchargers, Baird became interested in Formula One. Paul Emery acquired the straight-eight Clemons engine from the Brooklands Duesenberg and used the original Emeryson Special as the basis for a Formula 1 car. The chassis was lengthened and the Clemons-Duesenberg engine installed, with a bigger and stronger E.N.V. gearbox. A shapely aluminium body was built, attached to a tubular framework by aircraft fasteners, and Paul Emery and Bobby Baird drove this 4¼-litre unblown special in a number of Formula 1 races during 1948. It ran in the Jersey Road Race and the British Empire Trophy race in the Isle of Man among others.

When Baird changed his allegiance to Grand Prix Maserati cars the Emeryson-Duesenberg was sold to his compatriots. They used it in Irish hill-climbs and air-

Paul Emery with the Clemens-powered Emeryson Special in the Isle of Man in May, 1948. (Guy Griffiths)

field races for a number of years, during which time the chassis was shortened and the Singer IFS was removed and replaced by 2½-litre Riley wishbones and torsion bars. It was more or less run to death and then taken apart and finally returned to England in a box. The engine was salvaged and put back into the Duesenberg chassis, from which it had been taken, while the remains of the Emeryson Special were 'hung up in the roof' as one of racing's curios.

Ferguson P99

Project 99 of the Ferguson Research company in Coventry was a Research and Development Test Vehicle to demonstrate and develop four-wheel drive for high-performance cars and racing cars. Apart from its ability to demonstrate the advantages of 4-W-D it was also a successful single-seater racing car.

It was designed by Claude Hill and the chassis was able to accommodate a 1½-litre or 2½-litre Coventry Climax 4-cylinder racing engine. It had a finely honed, multi-tubular space-frame of very small-diameter steel tubing, with double wishbone and coil spring damper unit layout at each corner, to give all-round independent suspension. At a time when everyone had followed the Cooper mid-engine fashion, the Ferguson P99 had its engine mounted in the front, canted and angled to the left to allow a very low seating position and low frontal area. The drive passed through a 5-speed constant-mesh Ferguson gearbox and then divided through a central differential unit to shafts running fore and aft to Ferguson differential axle units, with short constant-velocity jointed shafts to each wheel. The system of four-wheel drive was the Ferguson patented three-differential layout, with the drive permanently engaged to all four wheels. Dunlop disc brakes were used and these were operated by the Dunlop 'Maxaret' system of anti-lock operation. The organizational force behind the P99 was the retired racing driver Major Tony Rolt and he loaned the car to his friend Rob Walker so that his Pipbrook Racing Team could run it in selected events.

With 1500 cc Coventry Climax engine the Ferguson P99 was driven to victory in the 1961 Gold Cup race at Oulton Park by Stirling Moss. (T. C. March)

The first race in which it appeared was the Inter-Continental event at Silverstone in 1961, where it ran in 2½-litre form. The following week it appeared in the British Grand Prix, in 1½-litre form, and driven by Jack Fairman it really showed its potential in the rain. In September it ran in the Gold Cup Race at Oulton Park, driven by Stirling Moss, and had a runaway victory on a wet-and-dry track, against strong opposition.

After this the P99 was used for the purpose for which it was built, namely research and development work on vehicle handling and stability, four-wheel drive and anti-lock braking, amassing a vast amount of data for Ferguson Research and the braking division of Dunlop. It probably covered more miles on research than it ever did in racing.

In 1963 it raced in the Australian and New Zealand Tasman race series, with 2½-litre Coventry Climax engine, driven by Graham Hill and Innes Ireland. The following year it was loaned to Peter Westbury, who convincingly won the British Hill-climb Championship, giving ample proof of the value of 4-W-D on acceleration and traction. Having served its purpose as a high-speed research vehicle, P99 was kept at Ferguson Research Ltd until Tom Wheatcroft opened his Donington Collection of single-seater racing cars, whereupon Tony Rolt presented him with Project 99 to be put on permanent display alongside some much less successful 4-W-D racing cars.

'Genuine'

Acknowledgements to The Donington Collection.

Ferrari

Enzo Ferrari built his first Grand Prix single-seater in 1948 and he has been building Grand Prix cars ever since, so it is probable that he has built more single-seater racing models than anyone else. His first Grand Prix car was a rather vicious little beast, with a very short wheelbase, swing-axle rear suspension and a 'peaky' V-12 1500 cc supercharged engine. However, development was rapid and the original Tipo 125 soon had a longer wheelbase, de Dion rear suspension and better weight distribution and this started a long line of very successful Grand Prix cars.

The heart of that first car in 1948 was its beautiful little V-12 engine in which rpm was the keynote, and on its first appearance the world became conscious of the 'Ferrari Sound'. To this day racing engines have been Enzo Ferrari's true love and he has never made dull and uninteresting ones. If Ferrari makes an engine it is usually good, though there have been one or two that did not come up to the high standard expected.

After following the 1500 cc supercharged route for the 1947–51 Grand Prix Formula, to its inevitable complicated end of multiple camshafts, two-stage supercharging and more and more rpm, all in an endeavour to catch Alfa Romeo, Ferrari stopped supercharged engine development. He took the other Formula limit of 4500 cc unsupercharged, using his sports car and production car knowledge, and quickly built a new Grand Prix engine. It started at 3.3 litres, was enlarged to 4.1 litres and then to the full 4.5 litres, all with a row of downdraught Weber carburettors in the vee.

This project started in 1950 and by the end of the season the 4½-litre unblown Tipo 375 Ferrari Grand Prix car had the measure of the all-conquering Tipo 158 Alfa Romeo team. 1951 saw the ultimate expression of the unblown part of the Formula 1 rules in the shape of the V-12 Ferrari engine with twin sparking plugs to each cylinder and three special 4-choke downdraught Weber carburettors. The Alfa Romeo team were finally beaten, ironically by an earlier single-plug version of the 4½-litre Ferrari at the British Grand Prix at Silverstone in mid-1951. But for a wrong tyre choice in the final race, Ferrari's Alberto Ascari would have won the World Championship with the Tipo 375.

Even though Scuderia Ferrari were involved in a busy Formula 1 season, they found time to develop F2 cars, similar in chassis and suspension design, but using 2-litre unblown engines to comply with the F2 limits. After trying V-12 and 4-cylinder versions they settled on the latter, and the Tipo 500 was a rugged twin-cam 4-cylinder. When Formula 1 died in 1952 from lack of support, the World Championship races were switched to Formula 2, and needless to say Ferrari was all ready for it. In 1952 and 1953 the Tipo 500 Ferrari literally swept the board, with only the odd victory here and there going to any other manufacturer.

While running this strong racing programme Ferrari often sold redundant works cars to selected customers, and occasionally let them have new cars that were almost to factory-team specification. One very special customer was Tony Vandervell, the owner of VP Products, the manufacturers of VP shell-bearings, which Ferrari was using in his engines. After buying/loaning a short-wheelbase and a long wheelbase supercharged 1500cc car, Vandervell went the big unblown

Peter Whitehead's 1½-litre Tipo 125 supercharged V-12 Ferrari in the paddock at
Silverstone in 1949. (Guy Griffiths)

The Ecurie Espadon-entered 2-litre Ferrari Tipo 166 V-12 Formula 2 car of Peter Hirt in the 1952 British Grand Prix. (T. C. March)

Alberto Ascari's 4½-litre Tipo 375 Ferrari in the 1951 British Grand Prix. (Guy Griffiths)

route with a 4½-litre V-12 Ferrari, which he modified sufficiently to justify renaming it the 'Thin Wall Special'. The name Thin Wall was VP Products trade name for their thin-shell bearings. The Vanwall racing team developed their first 4½-litre Ferrari in line with the factory cars, and in 1952 it had a new twin-plug V-12 engine, and the latest chassis frame. Suspension, brakes, transaxle and so on were changed over to the new chassis frame and a second 'Thin Wall' Special evolved, which raced in Formule Libre events up to 1954. The Thin Wall Special Ferrari was probably the most powerful racing car on the British circuits until 1955, being well able to deal with the V-16 B.R.M. with its reputed 450 bhp. The Vandervell-developed Ferrari engine gave over 400 bhp in a very drivable chassis.

Ferrari pursued his 4-cylinder theme from Formula 2 into the new Formula 1 of 1954, with its 2½-litre engine limit. The 1953 works cars were remodelled into the Tipo 625 with the 2½-litre 4-cylinder engines. In addition his design team tried a new concept with the Tipo 553 in which all the weight was kept within the wheelbase in the interests of low polar-moment of inertia, a concept that Con-

Peter Collins with the highly developed and much modified Ferrari 'Thin Wall Special' battles to hold off the Maserati 250F of Moss at Aintree in September, 1954. (Motor)

naught had followed since 1949! The Ferrari was tried out as a 2-litre Formula 2 car to start with and then became the Formula 1 car for 1954 in 2½-litre form. It carried its fuel in pannier tanks each side of the cockpit and had a high, humpy tail, so was nicknamed 'Il Squalo' (The Shark). At first the team drivers did not like this new design, for it spelt uncontrollable *understeer* in contrast to previous Ferraris that had a basic characteristic of controllable *oversteer*, or vintage-style tail-out handling. A compromise was reached for 1955 and the revised car became known as the Tipo 555, or 'Super-Squalo', but by this time the 4-cylinder engine concept was out-dated and it could barely cope with the 6-cylinder 250F Maserati, let alone the Lancia V-8 and the Mercedes-Benz W196 fuel-injected straight-eight.

By 1955 the Scuderia Ferrari were in the doldrums, but then the Lancia racing team of D50 cars was given to Ferrari to uphold Italian prestige. For two years, in 1956 and 1957, the Ferrari-modified Lancias, that became known as Lancia-Ferraris, kept the Ferrari name in the forefront of Grand Prix racing. Ferrari now

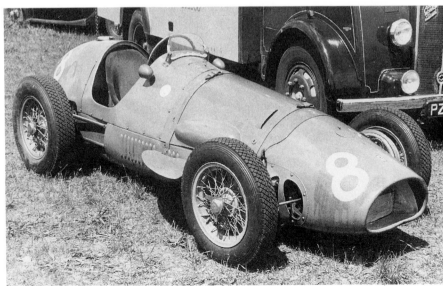

Bobbie Baird's private Tipo 500 Ferrari in the paddock at Snetterton in May, 1953. (Guy Griffiths)

This Tipo 625 Ferrari was driven into second place in the 1954 British Grand Prix at Silverstone by Mike Hawthorn. (LAT)

Mike Hawthorn with the Tipo 625, rebodied for 1955, in that year's British Grand Prix at Aintree. (T. C. March)

Mike Hawthorn with the Tipo 553 'Squalo' Ferrari on his way to a win in the 1954 Spanish Grand Prix at Barcelona. (The Geoffrey Goddard Collection)

Eugenio Castellotti with the modified Lancia-Ferrari in the 1956 French Grand Prix at Reims. He finished second. (Günther Molter)

In the 1957 British Grand Prix at Aintree Luigi Musso finished second with this Lancia-Ferrari. (T. C. March)

had his back to the wall, with strong opposition from B.R.M., Maserati and Vanwall, so there was no time for supporting customers with ex-factory cars, and none of the V-8 Lancia-Ferraris ever escaped into the outside world.

The Lancia concept had reached the end of its development by the end of 1957, so Ferrari started off an entirely new route, with smaller and lighter cars built around a new V-6 engine. Ferrari's son Dino was involved in the design of this new V-6 engine, along with Vittorio Jano, and after his sudden death through illness, the whole V-6 project was given the name 'Dino'. It began as a Formula 2 project of 1500 cc, going up through 1.8, 2.2, to 2.4 litres, to become the spearhead of the Formula 1 team for 1958. The Ferrari Dino 246 took the team right through to the rear-engined revolution of 1959–60, and was the last traditional front-engined Grand Prix Ferrari to be built.

The early Grand Prix Ferraris that were sold were not very successful, and there was not a strong customer back-up service on development from the factory racing department, unlike Maserati with their 250F. Consequently, few of them sustained their pace and lasted to become Historic racing cars. The only 4½-litre that kept on racing was the 'Thin Wall Special', and G.K.N./Vandervell kept the second version in full working order, giving demonstration runs with it now and then right through to 1986, when it was sold to Tom Wheatcroft along with the Vanwall cars. Others became very obsolete by 1953 and were allowed to deteriorate, or were made into 'specials' for some other form of racing. Two or three have been restored, though no one uses them in anger in Historic racing, as they do with 250F Maseratis or Cooper-Bristols, which is a pity. The 1954–55 cars were outclassed when they were new, so there is no incentive to do much in the way of res-

In the 1957 German Grand Prix, Mike Hawthorn (Lancia-Ferrari) leads team-mate Peter Collins. (Motor)

Mike Hawthorn with the Ferrari Dino 246 in practice for the 1958 Moroccan Grand Prix at Casablanca. (Edward Eves)

toration or resurrection for Historic racing. There are some of the 4-cylinder Ferraris about in museums, notably the Donington Collection, the Biscaretti Museum and the Schlumpf Collection.

All the Lancia-Ferraris were broken up by the racing department at the end of 1957, the chassis frames being cut up and scrapped, the bodywork, tanks, wheels, brakes and so on being scrapped and only the engines and gearboxes being kept. These were sold off to collectors many years later as curios. A similar fate befell the Dino 246 cars when Ferrari joined the mid-engine fashion, though two cars did escape the scrap-man. One went to Luigi Chinetti, the USA Ferrari importer, purely as an incomplete exhibition car, and another was rebuilt by the factory with a 3-litre V-12 sports-car engine installed in place of the V-6 unit. This was for a private customer for use in Tasman racing in Australia and New Zealand. It was later made into a Sports/GT car, but was then retrieved and brought to England to be rebuilt into single-seater form, to make potentially the fastest Historic Ferrari racing car.

The New York show-car was acquired by an English collector and was completed and made to perform as it did originally, and became a feature of Historic racing. During the rebuild it was used to provide patterns for building two 'Facsimiles' of reasonable accuracy. One of these retained the production-based Dino 246 engine that was built into it, and people often try to convince themselves that it is a genuine Dino 246 Formula 1 car. The other 'Facsimile' was sold to an Italian collector, who 'found' a 1500 cc Dino engine unit, which he installed in place of the

By 1960 the Dino 246 was outclassed. Wolfgang von Trips drove this car into sixth place in the British Grand Prix at Silverstone. (T. C. March)

2½-litre, and the car now masquerades as the 1957 Ferrari Dino Formula 2 car, which it patently is not.

No doubt one day a 'Facsimile' of a Lancia-Ferrari will appear, but it will be a misguided effort, as the original Lancia-Ferraris were not very good when they were new. It would make more sense to build a 'Facsimile' of a D50 Lancia, except that in the world of exotica the name Lancia does not have the same charisma as Ferrari.

Single-seater Ferraris in Historic racing are pretty rare, and those that do appear have little historic background of any great value, even the Tasman V-12 Dino; usually the ones mouldering away in museums have the history and are genuine.

Acknowledgements to *Ferrari* by Hans Tanner and Doug Nye.

Fiat

In the Edwardian period Fiat were very strong in racing, their 1910 cars with 10½-litre 4-cylinder engines being particularly successful. They returned to Grand Prix racing in 1921 with a 3-litre car in the idiom of the immediate post-war thinking, but it was not a great success. However, for the new 2-litre Formula in 1922 they produced a very advanced 6-cylinder which others were quick to copy the following year, but Fiat were already one step ahead, as their 1923 car was a brand new 8-cylinder to which they applied supercharging. At first they used a vane-type of blower, but then changed to a Roots paddle-type, and in this form the Fiat won the Italian Grand Prix. It was the first Grand Prix victory by a supercharged car.

As with their 1922 6-cylinder engine, their supercharging led the way for others to copy. They withdrew from the Grand Prix scene in 1924, but this did not stop them building experimental racing engines, one such being a 2-stroke 12-cylinder with opposed pistons.

Pietro Bordini drove this 'double-six' Fiat Tipo 806 into first place in the very short 1927 Milan Grand Prix at Monza.

In 1927 they returned to Grand Prix racing with another 12-cylinder engine, supercharged naturally, and this had two rows of six cylinders mounted side by side with two crankshafts geared together. This engine gave a remarkable 175 bhp at 7500 rpm, which was outstanding for the time, but after winning one race with it, Fiat again withdrew, this time for good. They never appeared in Grand Prix racing again.

Their engineering expertise was outstanding, and had they put as much effort into actually racing as Delage, Bugatti or Alfa Romeo did we may have seen the whole history of Grand Prix racing reading very differently.

Frazer Nash

Frazer Nash production was geared principally to the manufacture of sports cars, though many of them were eminently suited to racing, and quite a number were made into single-seater racing specials. The chain transmission, with a separate chain for each speed (or gear), from a cross-shaft, meant that the Frazer Nash chassis was ideal for a variety of engines. Indeed, the manufacturers themselves used many different types of engine over the years.

The Isleworth factory built three pure single-seater racing cars, using their own single overhead-camshaft 4-cylinder engine, the first of these being unblown and running on two S.U. carburettors, while the other two used the twin-Centric supercharger layout of the production Shelsley model. SS1, the first car, was built for the Hon. Peter Mitchell-Thomson in 1934, and after racing at Brooklands and Donington Park it was sold to Australia, where it still resides. The second car was chassis 2155, built for Adrian Thorpe in 1935, which later became the 'works car' driven so successfully by A. F. P. Fane. It was this car that broke the Shelsley Walsh record in 1937 and was active in VSCC events for a very long time, before retiring into the Donington Park Racing Car Museum. The third single-seater to leave the Isleworth factory was a sister car to that of Thorpe/Fane and was chassis

A 1935 Frazer Nash single-seater seen at the Luton Hoo Speed Trial in March, 1948. (Guy Griffiths)

The Frazer Nash 'Norris Special' driven by F. A. Norris at Shelsley Walsh hill climb in September, 1948. (Guy Griffiths)

2164, built to the order of the Hon. Peter Aitken. He did not use it a great deal, and after the war it became active in hill-climbs, but gradually got 'used up' and dismantled. With the resurgence of interest in vintage and Historic racing, 2164 was resurrected and totally rebuilt, to become 'Authentic' rather than 'Genuine' like the other two cars, and is a frequent competitor in VSCC racing to this day.

Among the many single-seaters built on Frazer Nash chassis, some of which are featured elsewhere in this book under their own names, was the Norris Special. This was built by Frank Norris, a North London enthusiast, who was very active in the immediate post-war years. He took a supercharged 1½-litre Alvis 4-cylinder engine from a front-wheel-drive Alvis sports car, turned it through 180 degrees

R. G. J. Nash at the wheel of the Frazer Nash 'Terror'. (The Geoffrey Goddard Collection)

R. G. J. Nash with the Frazer Nash 'Union Special' at Lewes in 1939. (The Author)

and coupled it to the Frazer Nash bevel-box by a normal clutch and propshaft. Moving the driving position into the centre of the chassis, he fitted a neat single-seater body and pointed tail, and with a fair amount of tuning to the Alvis engine, he had himself a fast and exciting sprint and hill-climb car. The car has weathered the years well and is still very active in the vintage world, occasionally appearing as a road-going sports car, fitted with mudguards, silencer and number plates.

The most famous single-seater Frazer Nash special is the one built originally by Archie Frazer Nash, and known as 'Terror'. Archie sold it to R. G. J. (Dick) Nash, no relation, who was very successful with it in the early 1930s in every form of competition from Brooklands races to dirt-track racing. From Nash it went through many hands and eventually got 'used up' and the bits passed to various special builders. Some of the bits eventually formed the basis for a 're-incarnation' in the form of Terror III, in acknowledgement of the changes in its life since it was built in the Kingston works.

After he parted with 'Terror' Dick Nash built himself a new single-seater Frazer Nash, using a 1934 frame and axles and installing a Shelsley model power unit. This was the single overhead camshaft Frazer Nash 4-cylinder engine with two Centric superchargers mounted on the front. Nash made the car as slim as possible, with a polished aluminium body and a short stumpy tail. He built this at the time of the appearance of Auto Union in Grand Prix racing, so he called his car the Frazer Nash-Union Special. It was never as successful as his previous special, and the engine proved to be temperamental in the high state of tune that Dick Nash demanded.

It was in his workshop at Brooklands during the war when some German bombs fell on the track. Nash's shed received a direct hit and the Union Special was written off. A member of the VSCC claims to have unearthed some of the remains, and plans to 'resurrect' the Union Special, but it will need to be called Union Special II.

By 1952 AFN Ltd, the makers of the Frazer Nash cars, were well into a series of very successful 2-litre sports cars, powered by a special version of the 6-cylinder Bristol engine. This was the Le Mans Replica model, and a Mk 2 version appeared with narrow tubular chassis frame that just cried out to be made into a single-seater. Peter Bell commissioned just such a car for Ken Wharton to race, and

Ken Wharton with the Peter Bell-owned Frazer Nash Formula 2 single-seater in the 1952 International Trophy at Silverstone. (T. C. March)

chassis 421/200/172S was built at Isleworth as a Formula 2 single-seater. It was notable for the large air intake that ran from the nose, back along the top of the bonnet, to feed the three downdraught carburettors, which gave it the nickname of the 'Wharton Whale'. After an active 1952 season competing in a number of Grand Prix events the car passed to a clubman who turned it into a narrow two-seater sports car, with minimal road equipment. He registered it OPW 666 and kept it for many years, until it began to deteriorate and become almost derelict. It was then acquired by a Frazer Nash enthusiast who rebuilt it back to its 1952 single-seater condition, almost better than when it was originally built. It is very active in Historic racing today.

Following the Peter Bell car, two more single-seater Frazer Nashes were built, 421/200/179S for Irishman 'Dickie' Odlum, who competed with it in Irish races and hill-climbs, and 421/200/180S for Scotsman W. J. Skelly.

As the F2 Frazer Nash was born from the Mk 2 Le Mans sports car, it was not surprising that they should be made into sports cars after their useful racing life was over. The Odlum car has been rebuilt as a Le Mans Mk 2 and has taken the surplus registration from the 'Wharton Whale', OPW 666, while the Skelly car has been registered ECN690 and is also in Mk 2 Le Mans sports car form.

In the days of the 2-litre Formula 2 for International racing the Le Mans Replica Frazer Nash, or the Mk 2, could be run as a racing car by the simple expedient of removing the mudguards, lights, passenger seat and so on. Two drivers who did this, in order to use their sports cars in British F2 races, were Tony Crook and Bob Gerard, which is why it might appear that Frazer Nash built more than three single-seater Formula 2 cars.

Acknowledgements to AFN Archives.

Freikaiserwagen

This special really is the 'Executioner's axe'. With four new heads and three new handles, a continuous history, and one owner, the question is 'Is it the original axe?' The answer, of course, is no, but it is genuine. The Freikaiserwagen is exactly the same; three different chassis frames, two different engines, three transmissions, two distinct configurations, and one owner. Yet it undoubtedly remained the Freikaiserwagen throughout its life.

It was built as a sprint and hill-climb car in 1936 by David Fry and Dick Caeser, who both came from the Bristol area. This was the time of the famed Auto Union racing cars, with the engine mounted behind the driver, which Dr Porsche designed and initially called the P-Wagen. The two West Country friends schemed up their special on the same lines, with the engine behind the driver, and they made a Germanic play on their names and created the Frei-Kaiser-Wagen. They took a simple G.N. chassis, with its chain transmission, and added the front suspension from a Morgan three-wheeler, which was independent by sliding pillars and coil springs. A vee-twin Anzani engine was mounted transversely and coupled more or less directly to the G.N. bevel-box. The driver sat in front of the engine, quite low as there was no propshaft to get in the way.

David Fry's cousin Joe joined the team and became the regular driver of the car as he was small and light, compared to the burly owner of the car.

In 1937 the Freikaiserwagen appeared in rebuilt guise, so that it could have been called Freikaiserwagen 2, but it wasn't. It was now powered by a very potent vee-twin racing 1100 cc Blackburne engine that came from Robin Jackson of Brooklands fame. This unit had been prepared for record breaking but had never been used, and running on alcohol fuel it was good for about 70 bhp, which made the skimpy little car very lively. The fearless Joe sat right at the front of the chassis, his feet just behind the cross-tubes of the front suspension, and behind his head was

Joe Fry at the wheel of the Freikaiserwagen at Shelsley Walsh hill climb in September, 1948. (Guy Griffiths)

the fuel tank of aerofoil section, having come from a light aircraft. In the interests of creating some semblance of *understeer*, or to combat violent *oversteer*, narrow-section front tyres were used and the largest-section rear tyres they could accommodate. It was not long before more power was needed, so a Marshall supercharger was applied to the vee-twin Blackburne engine. By 1939 it was becoming one of the leading competitors in British sprints and hill-climbs, but just before the war put a stop to racing, Joe had a big accident in the car and nearly wrote it off.

After the war it was rebuilt, using the chassis and Morgan front suspension from the Watkins-Nash, another special built by a Bristolian. The supercharged vee-twin Blackburne 1100 cc engine was retained and the G.N.-Frazer Nash chain transmission. Robin Jackson took a keen interest in the engine development and, as over 100 bhp was being obtained, some serious strengthening of the internal components was needed, with redesigned moving parts. For the 1949 season David Fry produced the ultimate Freikaiserwagen, built on a new tubular chassis frame designed by Dick Caeser for his 500 cc Formula 3 Iota car. By this time Jackson had developed a two-stage supercharger layout, with two Marshall blowers and with very little of the original Blackburne engine left, apart from the angle of the vee and the 1100 capacity. Power was now in the order of 120 bhp and the whole car weighed around 600 lb. The engine was still mounted amidships, but was now fore-and-aft, driving through a Norton motorcycle gearbox and clutch to the chassis-mounted final drive, which contained a Z.F. limited-slip differential. Rear suspension was independent by exposed drive-shafts on the swing-axle principle using rubber strands in tension as the medium. The front end was still basically Morgan, with light coil springs and hydraulic shock absorbers. Joe Fry was still seated in a simple aluminium bucket-seat in front of the engine.

In this form the Freikaiserwagen was capable of taking on anyone in sprints and hill-climbs, and it broke the famed Sheisley Walsh record in 1949. Sadly, this exciting car ended its history in 1950. Joe Fry crashed at the Blandford hill-climb and was killed, and cousin David never had the heart to rebuild it. The wreckage was put away for ever.

Gordini

Amédée Gordini, a Frenchman of Italian origin, was known to his friends and colleagues as 'The Magician', for he seemed to be able to conjure up things from nowhere, and whether it was horsepower, financial support, materials, design work or manufacture, he seldom failed when all looked lost. He inspired those who worked for him so much that they often achieved the impossible. When his new 2-litre 6-cylinder Formula 2 car was late in being completed in 1952, and time had run out for the transporter to get to Berne in time to qualify for the Swiss Grand Prix, Jean Behra, one of his drivers, had the tank filled with their special racing fuel, got the mechanics to push-start the car and drove non-stop from Paris to the Swiss frontier at Basle. There he talked his way into Switzerland and got the Swiss Customs officials to push-start the racing car, and he arrived in Berne in time for practice.

Gordini started in racing in the 1930s with a Simca-Fiat-based sports car, modifying it extensively to his own tuning ideas. It was not until 1947 that he was able to branch out into single-seater racing with slim little cars built around Simca-Fiat sports car components. These were 1100 cc 4-cylinder cars, one of which left the factory team in 1948 and eventually ended up in England. Today it resides in the Donington Museum, a prime example of Gordini's early single-seaters.

Once into single-seater cars Gordini's development and production was remarkable for such a small concern, especially as he carried on an equally prolific sports car racing programme, both as a factory team and for customers. The whole Gordini concern was very dependent on paying its way with appearance money, prize money and bonus money from fuel and tyre companies, and for this reason both sports and Formula cars were kept racing continuously, even at the expense of losing reliability at times.

His 1100 cc cars had pushrod ohv engines, basically Fiat, but soon Gordini

The 1100 cc Simca-Gordini with Bira at the wheel. He enjoyed a fine run of success with these cars in 1947. (LAT)

Jean Behra with the 2½-litre Gordini in the 1954 British Grand Prix at Silverstone. (T. C. March)

cylinder heads with better valve gear appeared; engine capacity grew to 1500 cc, and the engines became pure Gordini. By 1950 the little 1½-litre cars were performing well enough to add superchargers to them and qualify for Formula 1 Grand Prix races, not with any hope of winning against the sophisticated opposition from Ferrari, Maserati and Alfa Romeo, but they made up the field and gained the team a lot of experience, as well as much-needed appearance money. For the 1952 Formula 2 season entirely new cars appeared from the Paris factory and justified dropping the Simca part of the name, so they became simply Gordini. These cars were 2-litre 6-cylinder all-aluminium racing engines, with three double-choke Weber carburettors and twin overhead camshafts. The Achilles heel of the Gordini was the light back axle, sprung on torsion bar springs, but without independence. Half-shaft breakages, differential breakages and hub failures were

The straight-eight Gordini of Robert Manzon in the 1956 British Grand Prix at Silverstone; he finished eighth. (T. C. March)

rife as the new engine developed more and more power. To have adopted independent rear suspension or the more popular de Dion suspension would have meant a major redesign, which Gordini could not afford.

Throughout 1952 and 1953 the 6-cylinder Gordinis were well in the running at times in Formula 2 and able to challenge strongly while they lasted. In 1952 Jean Behra in a Gordini beat the might of Ferrari and Maserati in a memorable Reims Grand Prix. Although Gordini did not market his racing cars, he did sell one or two to special customers, and was quick to make a deal with a wealthy amateur to allow him to buy his way into the team with an extra works car. By the end of Formula 2 in 1953 resources were becoming very stretched and the cars began to get left behind in top-class racing. When the new 2½-litre Formula started in 1954 Gordini tried to carry on, using a 2½-litre version of his 6-cylinder engine, but the power and speed provided was completely beyond the capabilities of the chassis, suspension and rear axle.

The 2½-litre Grand Prix 6-cylinder was only meant as a stop-gap, as Gordini had an entirely new car on the stocks, but a shortage of money was delaying its completion. The first of the new cars was not ready until the end of the 1955 season, and by then the design was out-dated. It was a 2½-litre straight-eight version of the well-tried Formula 2 engine, mounted in a new chassis with independent suspension to all four wheels by a Watts linkage system of swinging arms to carry the wheel hubs, and torsion bars springs all round. The design broke new ground in having what became known as a 'bluff-nose', whereby the air intake cowling in front of the radiator ran full width across the front, partially protecting the tyres from the air-stream and merging into a full-width body between the front and rear wheels.

Two of the 8-cylinder Type 32 cars were built and they competed in Grand Prix racing in 1956, but were just too slow to keep up with the opposition and had lost that light, nimble characteristic of the earlier Type 16 cars. In 1957 Amédée Gordini had to pull out of Grand Prix racing before he went bankrupt.

In later years, after he retired, Gordini let Fritz Schlumpf have most of his racing and sports cars, including the two 8-cylinder cars. Christian Huet, a French journalistic friend of Gordini, acquired some of the 6-cylinder single-seaters, along with all the factory drawings and records, and in 1984 he published a fine tribute to Amédée Gordini in the form of a very large and very comprehensive book about the whole life of 'Le Sorcier' and his cars. It is a bible for anyone interested in Gordini, the man, the cars, or the racing team.

Other Gordini racing and sports cars have been preserved by various museums in France as a tribute to a French concern that did as much for French racing prestige as anyone. Apart from 16 cars in the Schlumpf museum in Mulhouse, Christian Huet has four in his private collection, the Bec Helloin museum has three, Serge Pozzoli has two, the Museum at Rochetaillée near Lyon has two, and Donington has one, while others have been scattered as far afield as the Argentine.

If a Gordini single-seater appears in Historic racing it can be fairly safely assumed that it will be 'Genuine'.

Acknowledgements to *Gordini—un Sorcier, une Équipe* by Christian Huet, Editions Christian Huet, Paris.

Gulf-Miller

Harry Miller must surely be the most famous and most prolific American designer of racing cars and racing engines. Many of his inventions were well before their time, and it took others to perfect them many years later. His 1½-litre and 2-litre straight-eight racing engines dominated American racing in the 1920s and his design features were copied by many people, even the hallowed Ettore Bugatti.

The car featured was Harry Miller's last great design, not great because it was successful, but because it was so forward-looking. It was designed specifically for the Indianapolis 500-mile race and was Miller's idea of an Auto Union, as perfected by Dr Porsche. He built a prototype which appeared for practice at Indianapolis in 1938, and he persuaded the Gulf Oil Corporation to finance a team of three cars for the 1939 Indy 500. The cars were built in Gulf Oil's research centre in Pennsylvania and appeared for qualifying in the spring of 1939. Gulf had insisted that the cars ran on their 81-octane No-Nox Ethyline petrol, which instantly put Miller at a horsepower disadvantage against rival cars running on alcohol fuel, but undeterred he set up the engines to use the straight petrol.

Normally everyone used alcohol fuel at Indianapolis, and Gulf's insistence on straight petrol for their cars was to be the direct cause of some nasty fires at the Speedway.

The Gulf-Miller design featured a 6-cylinder engine of 3 litres capacity, with twin overhead camshafts and fed by a centrifugal supercharger giving 20 lb boost. The engine was mid-mounted behind the driver, with the clutch on its forward end. This delivered power through a short shaft to the gearbox located below the driver's feet, and this in turn was coupled to the front-wheel-drive unit. Not content with this innovation of layout, Miller ran a shaft rearwards from the side of the gearbox, back alongside the engine to a rear-axle unit, and jointed shafts to the wheels. All four wheels were positively driven, and all four were independently sprung by transverse leaf-springs and small wishbone members, all enclosed in slim fairings. The 6-cylinder in-line engine was canted to the left at 45 degrees and the exhaust pipes rose vertically up through the tail. Later they fed into a collector box with a fishtail-like exit in the extremity of the tail.

In the interests of keeping weight distribution constant, fuel was carried in pan-

The 1939 rear-engined four-wheel-drive Miller with George Bailey at the wheel. Behind the car is Harry Miller. (The Author's Collection)

nier tanks slung along each side of the body. Radiators were mounted on each side of the stubby nose, air entering through the nose grille and exiting sideways. The shaft to the front-mounted gearbox, which was all part of the four-wheel-drive layout, meant that the driver sat rather high, so that this Miller design for Gulf was as tall as his earlier design for Ford had been low.

Years ahead of their time were Miller's disc brakes used on the Gulf cars, these operating on the plate-clutch principle rather than today's caliper system.

Although the cars ran at Indianapolis in 1939, 1940 and 1941, they were never really fast enough, being always down on horsepower due to having to use standard petrol. They also suffered a number of horrific accidents, due to the driver's having to acclimatize themselves to the 4-W-D handling. Hitting the Indy wall with a Gulf-Miller spelt disaster, for the pannier tanks would rupture and the volatile petrol ignited too easily, compared to methanol-based fuel. By 1941 the Indianapolis rules banned exposed fuel tanks, which meant that Miller had to encase his tanks in box-section side frames made from stainless steel.

Harry Miller died in 1943, and when Indy restarted in 1946 one of the cars reappeared, but was still not successful; nor was it the following year. The only notable achievement by a Gulf-Miller was a bout of record-breaking in 1940 at Bonneville, on the Salt Flats. It took Class D (2–3 litre) records at 158.446 mph for the flying 5 kilometres, 150.242 mph for 1 hour and 142.779 mph for 500 miles.

Acknowledgements to *The Miller Dynasty* by Mark L. Dees.

H.A.R.

Horace Richards was a Midlands enthusiast who raced Rileys just after the war, and this led him into special building. With the major races being to Formula 2 rules in 1952–53 Horace built himself a car to comply with the Formula, and used his initials to name it the H.A.R.

The chassis was built from large-diameter steel tubing on the 'ladder-frame'

principle, and he devised independent suspension for all four wheels using torsion bar springs. A 2-litre 6-cylinder Riley racing engine and gearbox were installed ahead of the driver, and a neat and straightforward contemporary-style body in aluminium was made.

The power output of the Riley engine, coupled with a fairly heavy car, was insufficient to match the lighter cars like the Cooper-Bristol or the more sophisticated ones like the A-type Connaught, so Horace had little success with his car. It is still in being, in a private collection in the Midlands.

There was a project to build a second H.A.R. to be powered by a supercharged 2.3-litre Bugatti engine, but it was never finished, though a complete H.A.R. rear end was grafted on to a Frazer Nash special at one time.
'Genuine'

H.R.G.

The H.R.G. firm built sports cars in a small factory at Tolworth in Surrey from 1935 to 1939, and continued after the war with basically the same car, changing over from the proprietary 1½-litre Meadows engine to the 1½-litre Singer engine.

When Formula 2 was introduced for International racing in 1948 the popular thing to do was to convert a successful sports car into a single-seater for this form of racing, the most notable being the B.M.W. 328.

The H.R.G. firm were not interested in doing this themselves, but they did not stand in the way of any private owner who had the idea. Peter Clark, a long-time competition driver of H.R.G. sports cars, built a single-seater using a shortened standard H.R.G. sports car chassis and installed a special 2-litre version of the new Standard Vanguard engine. The idea was to create a car suitable for Formula 2, but even in minor national races it was not competitive. The Vanguard engine could not be made to produce sufficient power, while the Standard 3-speed gearbox was pretty useless; added to this the H.R.G. chassis was very 'vintage' with hard-sprung rigid axles front and rear using leaf-springs, so that even on smooth aerodrome circuits it was not very good.

Although it was a neat and functional little car it was never a success and was a good illustration of the fact that you cannot make a silk purse out of a sow's ear. It did not even come close to being a 'silk sow' and was more of a 'dead duck'.

After running the car in small races and minor club events during 1949 the idea of the car becoming a competitive Formula 2 car was abandoned. The Standard Vanguard engine and gearbox were removed and a 1767 cc Lea-Francis 4-cylinder unit took their place, but even so it could not hope to compete in anything other than club racing; it did have a final fling in the BRDC International Trophy meeting at Silverstone in 1952, but it was so slow that it did not qualify to start.

It was then broken up and various useful components were dispersed to the four winds, the H.R.G. front axle still being in use on a standard H.R.G. sports car.

Another attempt at a single-seater H.R.G. appeared in sprints and hill-climbs in 1948, but with less ambitious objectives. This was built for Sir Clive Edwards, Bt., as a private venture for club events. The H.R.G. factory supplied a standard 1100 cc chassis for the project and into this was inserted a 1767 cc Lea-Francis 4-cylinder engine and gearbox. An H.R.G.-style radiator shell was used and single-seater bodywork was made, with a rounded rather than a pointed tail. Using the sports car chassis and steering meant that the steering wheel was slightly 'offset' in the single-seater cockpit.

Peter Clark with the Vanguard-powered Formula 2 H.R.G. at Blandford Camp in August, 1949. (Guy Griffiths)

The Lea-Francis engine was well developed to run on alcohol fuel and twin rear wheels were used to transmit the power, though the car suffered from a lack of weight on the rear of the chassis. Sir Clive Edwards competed with the car for a number of years, but was always handicapped by the odd size of the Lea-Francis engine, as he had to run in the 2000 cc class, and quite often in the 3000 class. Nevertheless, it represented a reasonably inexpensive sprint car with a satisfactory performance.

When Sir Clive withdrew it from the hill-climb scene it passed to other owners, and though it still exists it has not been seen for 20 years or more.

Acknowledgements to Ian Dussek (H.R.G. Owners' Association); *Motor Sport*, March 1949.

The Lea-Francis-powered H.R.G. single-seater driven by Sir Clive Edwards at Prescott hill climb in 1954. (NMM)

H.W.M.

When they left the Services after the war, George Abecassis and John Heath formed H.W. Motors, between Hersham and Walton in Surrey, hence the title of their firm. The object was twofold, one to make a living in the new and used-car motor trade and garage business, and the other to pursue their personal desires to go motor racing. Pre-war, Abecassis had been a noted driver of Alta racing cars, and he re-started with the Alta firm as soon as possible, as well as racing other cars.

Alta cars soon became part of H.W. Motors' workshop business, as they traded in Alta cars, raced them and modified them. After initial experiments on a pre-war Alta sports car, they built themselves an Alta-powered sports car with all-enveloping bodywork, and then a dual-purpose car which they called an H.W.-Alta. This had their own tubular chassis frame, I.F.S. by transverse leaf spring and wishbones, quarter-elliptic rear springs like an Alta, and an unsupercharged 2-litre 4-cylinder Alta engine, driving through an Armstrong Siddeley pre-selector gearbox. The driving position was set to the right of the prop-shaft and the body was a neat and simple affair tucked closely in around the mechanical components. Cycle-type mudguards and road equipment made it a fully-fledged sports car and it was registered NPA 5. It was easily stripped of its road equipment and was able to compete in the growing Formula 2 category of International racing.

This car was raced extensively during the 1949 season and became the prototype for a team of four new cars built during the following winter. The only major alteration to the design was the adoption of independent rear suspension, using a transverse leaf spring. When this ambitious project was begun it was intended to run the team as both sports cars and Formula 2 cars, but this idea was soon dropped and the H.W.M.s, as they were named, concentrated on a very full European season of Formula 2 racing.

Three of these 1950 cars formed the works team, and the fourth was sold to a private owner, who ran it in conjunction with the works team. Abecassis and Heath raced the cars, but many notable drivers were included in the team, among

John Heath's H.W.-Alta two-seater on its debut at Goodwood, Easter Monday, 1949. (Guy Griffiths)

The 1952 H.W.M. Formula 2 single-seater seen at Pau where it was driven by Lance Macklin. (The Author)

them Stirling Moss, Johnny Claes, Rudolf Fischer, Raymond Sommer and Lance Macklin.

The 1950 Formula 2 season was so successful, and the team created such a good impression in Europe, that they were encouraged to take a bold step in 1951. Four brand new cars were built, after making a mock-up, as pure single-seaters, with the driver sitting centrally above the propeller shaft, and all ideas of making the cars dual-purpose were abandoned. These new cars still used a tubular chassis frame, but new wishbone and coil-spring front suspension was built, and a de Dion layout was adopted at the rear. The financial budget was limited, so there was no possibility of using exotic materials, and the eventual cars were a bit on the heavy side for single-seaters, but they were rugged and strong, which was a bonus for the busy season that was planned. Engines were still Alta, and gearboxes remained pre-selector. With four cars available the team was able to cash in on dual entries on some weekends, two cars going to one race and the other two to another race in a different country.

For the 1952 season new cars were built, the major change being the use of coil springs at the rear in place of quarter-elliptic leaf springs. By 1953 the Alta engine was losing out on power, so a redesigned cylinder head was produced with the aid of Harry Weslake; these Weslake heads had the overhead camshafts driven by a train of gears from the back of the crankshaft, instead of the roller-chain system of the standard Alta engine. The pre-selector gearboxes were replaced by Jaguar units, but weight was always an H.W.M. problem, as the team could not afford special metals, nor could they make the cars fragile and suitable for airfield racing, as much of their season was spent on rough road circuits. In spite of the new cylinder head design, the power output was not sufficient to match the 4-cylinder Formula 2 Ferraris and the 6-cylinder Maseratis, and the H.W.M.s were getting left behind.

Lance Macklin with the 1953 H.W.M. in the British Grand Prix at Silverstone. (T. C. March)

They carried on until the end of the 1953 season, when Formula 2 ended, but hopes of competing in the new 2½-litre Grand Prix Formula in 1954 were thin. One of the 1953 cars was fitted with a 2½-litre Alta engine, and even tried with fuel injection, but on its outing in the French Grand Prix at Reims it was clearly outclassed by newer and stronger factory entries. Abecassis and Heath cut their losses and withdrew from single-seater racing and concentrated on Jaguar-powered H.W.M. sports cars.

None of these single-seaters was of much use for any other form of racing, even at club level, though some gravitated to Australia. Others became dismantled or modified into sports cars and apart from the prototype H.W.-Alta (NPA 5), which is still in good health, and one of the 1950 cars, there are only two single seaters still active in Historic racing. One is the 1951 model and the other a 1953 model, with the H.W.M.-Weslake version of the Alta engine.

Even when new the H.W.M.s were not particularly suited to short sprint-type racing on smooth airfields, so there is little encouragement for anyone to resurrect an H.W.M. for Historic racing.

Acknowledgements to *Motor Sport*, December 1950 and July 1980; *Alf Francis – Racing Mechanic*, G. T. Foulis Limited.

Halford Special

Major Frank Halford was a noted aero engine designer and in 1925 he designed and built himself a 1½-litre racing car engine. It had some advanced ideas, including exhaust-driven turbocharger, though this part of the design never got beyond the experimental stage. The engine which was built and raced was a 6-cylinder twin overhead camshaft unit with a Roots-type supercharger using two carburettors linked progressively.

This interesting engine was installed in an Aston Martin chassis of the type that the firm had used in their own Grand Prix cars, and the Halford car appeared at Brooklands as the A. M. Halford. Later this name was changed to Halford Special when it ran in the JCC 200-mile race at Brooklands in 1925. The following year it won two Brooklands Outer Circuit races and made its fastest lap at 109.94 mph. George Eyston drove it in the French Grand Prix at Montlhéry, but after that Halford withdrew it from racing and over the years it became dismantled and the components were scattered throughout the racing world.

Major Frank Halford with the Halford Special, photographed in 1925. (The Author)

In the 1970s James Cheyne began a monumental research and a hunt to trace all the parts. This he achieved over a number of years and the Halford Special was 'resurrected' to as near original as made no difference. It was truly the 'resurrection of the age', and the car is often seen in action in VSCC and other club events, a tribute to the owner's endeavours and a fine compliment to Frank Halford, one of Britain's most noted engine designers, with the long line of Napier aero engines to his credit.

Acknowledgement to Aston Martin Owners' Club Magazine.

Lancia

Vicenzo Lancia kept his firm out of serious racing for most of his life, but after his death his son Gianni took over the firm and had different ideas. As if sensing that the end of the family control was near, he embarked on a vigorous programme of racing, starting with saloon and GT cars from the Lancia range and progressing to a powerful factory programme of very special sports cars. This programme culminated in one of the most advanced Grand Prix cars ever to appear for a new Formula.

The D50 was designed by Vittorio Jano for the 1954 Grand Prix Formula and made a brief appearance at the end of that season, when two cars ran in the Spanish Grand Prix at Barcelona. This ultimate Lancia racing car bristled with advanced ideas and was beautifully executed, indicating the strength of Lancia's Research & Development department. With no weight restrictions or limits on size other than 2½-litre engine capacity, Jano had a free hand and the heart of the car was his four-camshaft V-8 of virtually equal bore and stroke, giving it very high rpm for the time. The engine formed the centre-section of the car, the front suspension frame being bolted to the front of the engine, and the rear of the engine being bolted to the cockpit bulkhead, in the manner of a modern Formula 1 car, but round the other way, as the Lancia D50 was front-engined. Such chassis frame as there was consisted of a finely executed space-frame in which the driver sat very low, the propshaft running diagonally across the floor of the cockpit to the 5-speed gearbox in unit with the final drive. Suspension was independent at the front by double wishbones and a thin transverse leaf spring; rear suspension was de Dion, also using a thin transverse leaf spring. Between the wheels, hung on tubular struts, were sponsons or panniers which carried fuel and the whole design concept was based on a low polar-moment of inertia to achieve neutral handling.

The factory team started the 1955 season with a flourish, winning races at Turin and Naples, with the powerful driver line-up of Alberto Ascari, Luigi Villoresi and Eugenio Castellotti. In May Ascari was killed while driving a sports Ferrari and his death virtually ended the Lancia team. Castellotti ran a car in the following Belgian Grand Prix, but then Gianni Lancia announced the takeover of the Lancia firm. The entire racing team was given to Enzo Ferrari and his Scuderia, that they

The Lancia D50 on its debut at the 1954 Spanish Grand Prix. This car was driven by Luigi Villoresi. (LAT)

might continue the fight for Italian supremacy in Formula 1. The cars, all the spares, the equipment and designs were handed over in a touching ceremony, but one car was retained by the Lancia factory. Ferrari received more than enough to ensure the continued running of a three-car team.

After an initial try-out in unchanged D50 form, the Scuderia Ferrari set out to improve the Lancias, and their development changed the original design so drastically that the whole concept of the D50 was lost. They were renamed Ferrari, and had it not been for the harsh bark of the high-revving V-8 Lancia engine, no one would really have known that the cars originated from Turin and not from Maranello. This programme ran through 1956 and 1957, after which the cars were broken up by the Ferrari factory.

It is fortunate that Gianna Lancia saw fit to keep back one original D50 car, for it was a landmark in Grand Prix design, and even today, more than 30 years later, it still bears close study. It is kept in running order by the Fiat-owned Lancia firm and occasionally is brought out to give demonstration runs.

In recent years an artisan in Turin has built a D50 'Facsimile' using some surviving original components.

Lister-Jaguar

In 1957 the Ecurie Ecosse took their team of D-type Jaguars direct from Le Mans to the Monza banked track in Italy to compete in an Indianapolis-type 500-mile race. A strong force of American cars and drivers came over, but the majority of Europeans boycotted the event; consequently the offer of the three D-type Jaguars was readily accepted by the organizers, even though they were in full Le Mans road-going trim. Naturally they could not match the speed of the American cars, but the rough concrete Italian track played havoc with the faster cars and the

The Ecurie Ecosse Lister-Jaguar single-seater photographed during practice for the Two Worlds Trophy race at Monza in June, 1958. (The Author)

Jaguars ran reliably, though a lot slower, and ended up winning a lot of money.

Misguided enthusiasm encouraged the Ecurie Ecosse to return the following year with a car built on the lines of the Indianapolis 'roadsters', which is to say, an offset single-seater with a relatively narrow body and exposed wheels. A Lister sports-car chassis was used, and a 3.8-litre Jaguar engine and gearbox were installed, but what was overlooked was that the American cars used 4.2-litre alcohol-burning Meyer-Drake engines, giving 400 bhp to the Jaguar's bare 300 bhp. With the same frontal area and drag, it was no contest and the Monza Lister-Jaguar was an also-ran before it even went out for practice.

The all-enveloping aerodynamic body of the sports D-type Jaguar was the real reason for its speed, rather than the power of its engine, so the Lister-Jaguar with the aerodynamics of a housebrick was not as fast. After this abortive outing the car was abandoned and eventually became rebuilt into a normal Lister-Jaguar sports car.

Later in its life it suffered a bad crash and had to have most of the chassis frame replaced and eventually became something of an abandoned wreck. With the revival and increase of Historic racing a new 'Facsimile' of the Monza car was re-created and became quite a powerful contender. Although the existing car is a good representation of the Ecurie Ecosse car it can hardly be accepted as the car which had the one lamentable outing in the 1958 Monza 500-mile event.

Lotus

Colin Chapman, founder and head of Lotus, took a long time getting into single-seater racing, preferring sports-car racing, unlike his contemporary John Cooper, who went straight into single-seater cars, albeit in a very minor category. By the time Chapman built a single-seater Lotus, for the 1957 Formula 2, he had already been assisting Vanwall and B.R.M. with chassis and suspension design for their Grand Prix cars.

The first single-seater Lotus was a diminutive little thing, with front-mounted 1500 cc Coventry Climax 4-cylinder engine, and the lightness of the structure bordered on the fragile. This was the Type 12, and while it was well suited to British short-circuit racing, it was not really of sufficient calibre for International events. The lightweight tubular space-frame would take a 2.2-litre Coventry Climax engine and one remarkable feat of the Lotus 12 was to finish fourth with Cliff Allison at the wheel in the Belgian Grand Prix in 1958 on the daunting Spa-Francorchamps circuit.

The Type 12 was followed by another single-seater in the Type 16, built to the same fragile concept, with its 2½-litre Coventry Climax engine canted over on its side to give a low body line. Both types of single-seater were endowed with a very delicate gearbox that was very small and light and in unit with the rear axle, the gear changing system being 'in line' rather than in an H-pattern gate, and the gear lever moving fore and aft on a positive-stop system like a motorcycle. Few drivers seemed able to adapt to this mechanism, which needed a velvet touch; the power of the 2½-litre engine was almost too much for it and the Lotus 'queerbox' became the Achilles heel of the Type 16.

Chapman spent too long trying to develop the Types 12 and 16, before he faced up to reality and put the engine behind the driver, as Cooper had been doing for

The Lotus 12 of W. Allen in the 1959 British Empire Trophy at Oulton Park. (T. C. March)

Bruce Halford's Lotus 16 in the 1959 British Empire Trophy at Oulton Park. (T. C. March)

some time. When he did, with the Type 18 (which is outside the scope of this book) it completed the revolution that Cooper had started and the face of Grand Prix racing was changed. Neither the Type 12 nor the Type 16 can be considered as successful single-seaters in the Lotus story and they were so flimsily constructed that they deteriorated rapidly when they became obsolete, even though the basic design was good. When a place was found for them in Historic racing, it was a case of digging up the bones that remained and 'Reconstructing' a single-seater Lotus, whether it be a Type 12 or a Type 16, and improving many of the design features, in the light of present-day knowledge, to make them reliable and raceworthy, especially in the gearbox region.

Acknowledgements to *Theme Lotus* by Doug Nye, Motor Racing Publications Limited.

M.G.

Thanks to the enthusiasm of Cecil Kimber, who ran the M.G. Car Company at Abingdon, the firm pursued a strong racing programme, principally by assistance to customers who wanted to race. Undoubtedly this support of racing built up an enviable reputation for the firm and until the take-over by the Nuffield Group in 1935 pure racing M.G.s could be bought 'over-the-counter'. Apart from the R-type, which was the M.G. Company's only single-seater racing car offered for sale, the other models stemmed from sports M.G.s and could be used for out-and-out racing events or in sports car events.

As they were all very susceptible to tuning and the company were not averse to making specialized components, many of the cars went through some serious development work, especially for racing on the Brooklands banked track.

K3 Magnette

The K3 was undoubtedly the most successful of all racing M.G. models and it was available in pointed-tail track-racing form, stripped of all unnecessary frills, or it could be had with mudguards, lights, dynamo, starter and so on, with a two-seater body with a small space behind the seats, and a slab-style fuel tank and rear-mounted spare wheel. While some of the K3 cars were raced in their standard pointed-tail racing form, with two-seater-width cockpit, even though there was only one seat, and that offset to the right for the driver, others were drastically altered into slim, streamlined single-seaters with a central driving position.

The production run of K3 cars was only 31 so that each one took on its own character, and though many of them became changed over the years, the basic character remained, for most of them had fairly consistent competition careers. There are a handful of very genuine cars still about, hardly altered at all from their original specification, but there are also some very good 'Facsimiles' about, made from non-K3 parts, altered and modified to look like the real thing. As there are some M.G. specialist/historians who retain all there is to know about the K3 series, these 'Facsimiles' do not get very far into the Historic scene, even though some look more original than original cars.

The K3 Magnette 6-cylinder engine of 1087 cc capacity was supercharged and had a single overhead camshaft driven by bevel gears and a vertical shaft from the front of the crankshaft, like all the other pre-Nuffield small M.G.s. The supercharger was mounted on the front of the crankshaft and protruded forwards under the radiator and between the chassis dumb-irons. An E.N.V. pre-selector gearbox was the standard fitting, and suspension was orthodox, by leaf springs, with friction shock-absorbers, the rear axle being underslung, with the chassis rails passing underneath. In racing form the engine ran to over 6000 rpm and was noted for its sharp crackle from the exhaust.

Q-type

This was a 746 cc supercharged 4-cylinder with the normal shaft-driven overhead camshaft and was an engine that was tuned to deliver remarkable power from such a small capacity. Like the K3 it was marketed as a ready-to-race pointed tail two-seater track car. The 750 cc class in British racing in the 1930s was very popular and many Q-types were converted into slim single-seaters, one of the fastest being the one raced by George Harvey-Noble and tuned by Robin Jackson. It lapped the Brooklands track at a class record of 122.4 mph. As with the K3 models the Q-type was built around standard production components, so it has not been difficult to

George Eyston at the wheel of a 1100 cc M.G. K3 photographed in 1934. (The Geoffrey Goddard Collection)

A works publicity shot of a 750 cc M.G. Q-type. (The Geoffrey Goddard Collection)

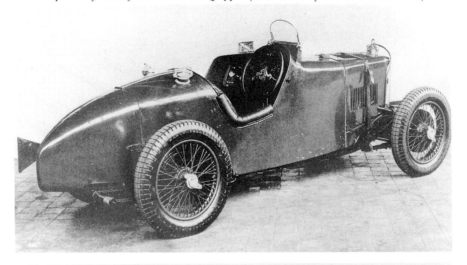

The 750 cc R-type M.G. with fully independent suspension by wishbones and torsion bars. (The Geoffrey Goddard Collection)

produce a 'Facsimile' of a Q-type. M.G. cars were always susceptible to suffering from special-builders, and genuine Q-types are few and far between.

R-type

This was the last model produced by the original M.G. Company before the Nuffield takeover. It was an audacious 'final fling' in the form of a pure racing single-seater, with a backbone chassis frame, independent suspension to all four wheels using torsion bar springs and a highly supercharged 750 cc engine, similar in layout to the Q-type engine. It was never fully developed, and the road-holding and cornering was not of the best. With M.G. withdrawing their racing support, those people who had bought R-types were severely handicapped in their efforts, and the model never made the mark on the racing scene that it should have made. Three cars were fitted with special cylinder heads having two overhead camshafts and inclined valves, as opposed to the normal layout of vertical valves in line below a single overhead camshaft. Like all the other racing M.G.s the R-type used an E.N.V. pre-selector gearbox and it was quite a neat and shapely little car. Although most of the small batch that were made have survived, they remain hidden away as far as Historic racing is concerned. To build a 'Facsimile' would tax the ingenuity of the most ardent specialist, and the end result could hardly be any better than the original cars, and they weren't very good!

Maserati

After working for the Diatto company, designing racing cars, Alfieri Maserati set up his own factory in Bologna to produce Maserati racing cars, adopting the Bologna Trident as the symbol for his badge. To begin with the primary object seemed to be to allow Alfieri to continue his career as a professional racing driver, and in his first year he built only three cars. The numbers increased as the years went by, but at no time could one consider any Maserati model as being in production.

Sports car racing and Grand Prix racing were Maserati's real love, and he was accompanied by his brother Ernesto, the two of them being accomplished drivers. In 1932 disaster struck when Alfieri had an accident, and while undergoing surgery he unexpectedly died, on 3 March, 1932, at the early age of 44. Ernesto and another brother, Bindo, carried on the traditions of their brother, in building and selling racing cars and competition sports cars. The firm flourished in the 1930s, and although Maserati were not quite the top marque in motor racing, they were always in with a shout, building up a strong following in the sporting world. The firm survived purely by racing, not attempting to move into any other branch of automobile manufacture.

Italy's involvement in the Ethiopian War in 1936 took some of the force out of the country's racing efforts, and the Maserati factory became hard pushed to make ends meet. Rather than allow things to get worse, Ernesto made a deal with the Orsi family in Modena for them to take over the Maserati firm. Adolfo Orsi was a successful industrialist and he took control of Maserati in 1937, with the agreement that Ernesto and his brothers, for Ettore had now become part of the firm, should stay on the payroll for ten years, thus ensuring that the design philosophies started by Alfieri, and ably carried on by his brothers, would continue along with the name.

1938 saw a resurgence in Grand Prix racing by the name Maserati and at the same time the beginning of new phase in Maserati activity in 'voiturette' racing. In 1939–40 everything was moved from Bologna to one of the Orsi factories in Modena, some 30 miles away. After the Second World War the newly constituted Maserati factory soon turned its activities from military projects to racing cars. The 1939 'voiturettes' continued to be raced and played an important role in the resumption of Grand Prix racing, especially as they were being made for sale, unlike the rival Alfa Romeo firm, who kept their racing cars for their own works team.

By 1947, when the ten-year contract expired, Ernesto Maserati had passed on

'Buddy' Featherstonhaugh on the banking at Brooklands in 1934 with an 8C–2500 Maserati. (The Geoffrey Goddard Collection)

his racing design philosophies to younger engineers, and he and his brothers left Modena and returned to Bologna to start up a new racing car firm of their own. They had to leave the name Maserati behind with the Orsi family, and though Maserati racing cars continued to be built and sold until 1958, they were no longer true Maseratis, and should have been called 'Orsis'. The real Maseratis were once again being built in Bologna by the Maserati brothers under the name O.S.C.A.

Regardless of this fact, the cars from Modena had all the hallmarks of true Maserati racing cars, and still carried the Bologna Trident on the badge, along with the name Maserati. The last single-seater Maseratis left the Modena factory in 1958, though the firm continued to make sports/racing cars, and are still in business today, under different management, making exotic GT cars and high-performance saloon cars.

Alfieri Maserati's first car in 1926 was called the Tipo 26, and was a supercharged straight-eight of 1500 cc. This was to affect the future design policy of the cars from Bologna, for although the firm built 4-cylinder, 6-cylinder and V-8 racing engines, the straight-eight cylinder layout became synonymous with the name Maserati. The earliest known 8-cylinder is a Tipo 26B of 1929 in the Biscaretti museum in Turin. The 8-cylinder theme continued through to 1934, culminating in the 8CM-3000, and along the way the capacity was enlarged to 2 litres, then 2.5 litres and finally 2.9 litres. In 1933 the first pure single-seater with the driver mounted centrally was introduced, the previous models having the driver sitting to the right of the prop-shaft. A diversion along the way had been a monstrous 4-litre Formule Libre car that used two 2-litre 8-cylinder engines in a narrow vee on a common crankcase with the crankshafts geared together. Two of these were produced in 1929, one of which was later given a smart Zagato two-seater sports body, and in this form it still exists in England. In 1932 a 5-litre version was produced, being in effect two 8C-2500 engines.

The slim single-seater 8CM-3000 was a strong contender for Grand Prix honours in 1933 and 1934 and a number of these cars are still about and active in Historic racing, while others rest in museums. Chassis No. 3010 is the car that was raced by Philippe Etancelin and is now in the Schlumpf Museum, and chassis No.

3018, that was the car raced by Nuvolari in the latter part of 1934, is in the Doning-ton Park Museum; these two are prime examples of the narrow and wide versions of the 8CM, respectively. Chassis Nos. 3011, 3013 and 3020 are alive and well and can be seen in action in Historic events. Others in the series of 17 *monopostos* that were built have either been destroyed long ago or lost in the mist of time. A new 'Facsimile' is being built that will no doubt try to assume one of the missing num-bers!

After a brief flirtation with a big 6-cylinder Grand Prix engine of 3.7 litres, which fitted into the 8CM chassis, and an abortive attempt at a V-8 of 4-litres ca-pacity in a new fully independently sprung chassis, the Maserati brothers turned their full attention to 'Voiturette' racing. The 3.7-litre car was known as the 6C-34 and two still exist, though the one that was in England was enlarged to 4 litres with a new cylinder block. A 'Facsimile' in sports car guise has been built, using some original components, this being built for a Swiss collector. The abortive V-8 engined car was known as the V-8RI and two were built in 1935, and two more in 1936. One, raced at Indianapolis, exists in remarkably complete form and another, owned by an English enthusiast, is being resurrected from a rather incomplete and sad state.

The Maserati 'voiturette' theme really began in the early days, when Alfieri built an 1100 cc version of his 8-cylinder Grand Prix car, but then interest lay dor-mant until after his death. Ernesto revived interest in 'voiturette' racing with what was in effect half of an 8CM, the little 4-cylinder 1500 cc engine being installed in a scaled-down 8CM single-seater chassis. This 4CM model was followed by a totally new 1500 cc car in 1936, which had a 6-cylinder twin-cam supercharged engine in a new slim chassis frame with independent front suspension by wishbones and longitudinal torsion bars. This was the 6CM, which was very effective in 1936, 1937 and 1938, and, as a variant, a 4-cylinder 1500 cc engine would also fit the frame, so you could have a 4C/6CM model.

Etancelin with his 8CM–3000 Maserati at Comminges in 1934. (The Geoffrey Goddard Collection)

One of the V-8RI Maseratis at Indianapolis. (The Geoffrey Goddard Collection)

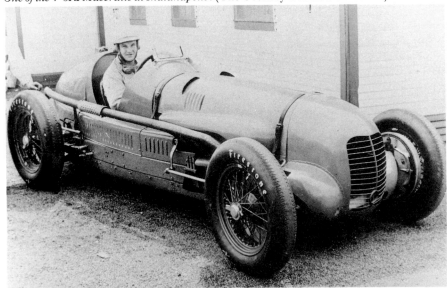

Wilbur Shaw won the 1939 and 1940 Indianapolis 500 Mile races with this 1938 Maserati 8CTF entered as the 'Boyle Special.' (The Geoffrey Goddard Collection)

In 1939 Ernesto Maserati started a new line of 1½-litre engines that was to carry right through to 1951, even after he had left the Orsi empire. The supercharged 4-cylinder twin-cam engine had four valves per cylinder and was of equal bore and stroke (78 × 78 mm) and ran to 7000 rpm, which was opening up a whole new field of engine development for the time. The chassis frame, of channel-section steel, was given rigidity by a massive alloy casting forming an oil tank that was fitted under the driving seat. Front suspension was similar to the 6CM, with wishbones and torsion bars, and the rigid rear axle was sprung on splayed-out quarter-elliptic leaf springs and located by radius arms. Somehow Maserati always managed to make their cars look right, the lines of the radiator cowls, the bodywork and the tail all blending in with a touch of artistry, and the 1939 4CL was no exception; it was a very pretty little car.

The new Formula for Grand Prix racing in 1938 which put an engine limit on

supercharged cars of 3 litres, encouraged the Maserati brothers to make a return to the big time. They produced the 8CTF, which clearly derived from their successful 'voiturette' designs. The straight-eight engine was effectively two 4C engines on a single crankcase, each block of four having its own supercharger, the two units being mounted one above the other on the front of the engine. The chassis and suspension was the forerunner of the forthcoming 4CL, except that the frame was built of tubes rather than channel steel, and the body lines were a development of the 6CM.

This new Grand Prix Maserati was immensely fast, and often gave a strong challenge to the German Mercedes-Benz and Auto Union teams. Sadly it lacked development and proved rather unreliable, being very fast for only a short time. Three of these big Maseratis were built and one went to the USA in 1939, to an American team who made it remarkably reliable. It won the Indianapolis 500-mile race in 1939, again in 1940 and was leading in 1941 when it broke down. It remained at Indianapolis for the rest of its life and today holds an honoured place in the Indianapolis Speedway Museum. The other two 8CTF cars also went to Indianapolis, with less success, and stayed on the American sporting scene for a long time. The three cars were numbered 3030, 3031 and 3032, and the third was the Indianapolis winner. The second car came to the UK for a long sojourn within the VSCC, being raced by Cameron Millar, but it has now been sold back to the USA. The first car has never left America since it was taken there in 1939.

An inevitable development was to build a Grand Prix version of the 16-valve 4CL, but this happened after Grand Prix racing had finished on the outbreak of war in 1939. One 8CL was built, on the same lines as the 8CTF, but with 16-valve cylinder blocks, making an impressive 32-valve straight-eight 3-litre. An Argentinian consortium bought the car for the 1940 Indianapolis 500, but it was unsuccessful. It then went to the Argentine, where it stayed until recent years, when it was purchased by a Japanese collector. A second 8CL was built after the war and that also went to the Indianapolis scene, where it was eventually broken up.

The immediate post-war period saw the 1939 4CL cars, and new ones built from 1946, dominating the racing scene, which had become regulated to 1½ litres. Maserati carried on their development of the 16-valve engine, using two-stage supercharging, and introduced a tubular version of the well-proven chassis. Shortly after the Maserati brothers left the firm, and Alberto Massimino took over the

Tazio Nuvolari in a Maserati 4CL in the 1946 Geneva Grand Prix. (The Geoffrey Goddard Collection)

design work, a completely revamped version of the 4CL appeared. This had the tubular chassis frame, the two-stage 16-valve engine, new front suspension using rocker-arms that compressed coil-springs (as Colin Chapman was to re-invent many years later on his Lotus cars), but retained the rigid rear end sprung on quarter-elliptic leaf-springs. This new model was the 4CLT/48, and as it made its debut at the San Remo Grand Prix in the spring of 1948, it became known as the 'San Remo' model.

This was to be the end of the line for the 4-cylinder Maserati theme that had started back in 1934, and though the 4CLT/48 gave way to an improved 4CLT/50 which ran to the end of the Formula in 1951, it was well past its prime by the end of its life. A run of 20 of these cars was built and while some have survived intact, others became modified and made into 'specials'. As they tended to have been 'driven into the ground' to the end of their active life, they have proved very difficult to resurrect or rebuild for use in Historic racing. Most racing car museums have an example on display, but the appearance of a 4CLT/48 in Historic racing is a rare sight.

Emmanuel de Graffenried drove this Platé-entered 4CLT/48 Maserati to victory in the 1949 British Grand Prix at Silverstone. (Guy Griffiths)

In 1950 a pair of 8CLT cars were built, which as their numbering suggests were 3-litre eight-cylinder versions of the 4CLT/48. They were originally planned for Indianapolis, but the idea was abandoned and they were sold to a New Zealand enthusiast. Only one seems to have survived and that is now back in Europe on the German museum scene, while the Maserati firm have the engine from the other car among their collection of memorabilia.

This was really the true end of the marque Maserati as started by Alfieri Maserati in 1926, and the final chapter was entirely under the Orsi influence. That is not to say that Adolfo Orsi and his son Omer did not keep up the traditions of the Maserati brothers. On the contrary, their racing programme from 1947 to 1958 was immense, and when they withdrew at the end of the 1957 season they had provided the car for Juan Manuel Fangio to win the World Championship, so the name Maserati in the world of Grand Prix racing ended on as high a note as was possible.

In 1952 the Orsi-Maserati line appeared as a 6-cylinder 2-litre Formula 2 car, which grew in stature throughout that year and into the 1953 season. These were the A6GCM, of which 12 were built, A6G coming from the 6-cylinder sports car, which started the 6-cylinder revival, and CM being the usual *Corsa Monoposto* (Racing Single-Seater). In 1954 there appeared a logical development in the form of the 250F, a 2½-litre 6-cylinder for the new Grand Prix Formula. From 1954 until 1957 the 250F was in production, both for the works team and for customers, and works development passed rapidly to customers. The series started in 1954 with chassis 2501 and went through to 2534, built to special order in 1958, though not all the numbers in the sequence were actually built. From the first to the last development was continuous, and the last of the series was undoubtedly the pin-

The 16-valve 4-cylinder engine of the 4CLT/48. (Guy Griffiths)

143

nacle of the 250F. Because of this continuous development, even for customer cars, few of the series fell by the wayside and many early cars were uprated. The 250F developed from a rather chunky, solid-looking single-seater to an elegant and sleek car that has stood the test of time. So attractive was the last of the series that most of the 'Facsimiles' that have been built have been modelled on the 1957 cars, and even some earlier cars that had to be brought back from the grave have been resurrected to look like 1957 models.

Among the last few cars built by the factory there were experiments made with a new V-12 cylinder 2½-litre engine, which fitted into the 250F chassis, though they were purely factory cars and none were sold off. After 2534 had been built and the factory closed their Grand Prix racing department, another version of the 250F was about to be built. It had got as far as the chassis frame stage, and this was bought by a group of enthusiasts in Modena and completed outside the factory, using an old 250F engine and transaxle, and appeared some time later as the Tec-Mec Maserati 250F. This ultimate expression of the Grand Prix single-seater from the Modena factory, while not being a pure Maserati, is interesting none the less and is preserved in the Donington Museum.

Acknowledgements to *Maserati – A Complete History* by Luigi Orsi and Franco Zagari, Libreria dell' Automobile, Milano; *Motor Sport* 1986.

History of the 250F

The A6GCM

During 1953 the Maserati works team had raced the 2-litre A6GCM model with tubular chassis frame, IFS by wishbones and coil springs, the 4-speed gearbox attached to the rear of the engine and an open propeller shaft to a rigid rear axle suspended on quarter-elliptic springs. To keep customers happy, while new 250Fs were being built, a number of A6GCM chassis were fitted with 2½-litre 250F engines. The 250F series had started on paper with chassis number 2501, so the idea was that the interim cars would take 250F numbers until the real 250F cars were available. This did not work out and merely added confusion. These interim cars were awful, for the transmission, suspension and roadholding were not able to cope with the power of a 2½-litre engine.

2501	A 1953 works 2-litre car with the engine replaced by a 2½-litre. Built for Roberto Mieres to begin the 1954 season. Had a rough life, crashed at Bordeaux, caught fire at Francorchamps and smashed up on a journey from Reims back to Modena, when it

was on the top deck of a two-tier transporter that overturned. As a new 250F was nearly ready for Mieres, this interim car was scrapped.

2502   Similar to the above, but gave the impression of being reliable because the owner, Jorge Daponte, did not drive it very hard. After only a few races Daponte took it back to South America, where it had a 'stock' American engine installed for National racing. It was recently retrieved less engine and resurrected in England with a built-up 250F engine.

2503   Third interim car built for Harry Schell. Raced by him for most of the 1954 season, then sold to Reg Hunt in Australia. Passed on to Kevin Neal and others. Came to the UK in 1970s, completely unspoilt, and passed to Ray Fielding.

2504   Built for Prince Birabongse for his use until new 250F was ready. Won the Grand Prix des Frontières at Chimay 1954. 250F engine removed and installed in a new 250F chassis, which took the number 2504. Interim car disposed of less engine to South America. Fitted with 'stock' American engine for National racing. Retrieved and brought to UK in recent years and resurrected.

2510   This number should have been a 250F for Baron der Graffenried, but it was never built. He retained this A6GCM/250F interim car and used it as a camera-car in the making of the film *Such Men are Dangerous*. It was then sold to a Swiss amateur, who used it in hill-climbs. Still in Switzerland, it resides in a museum.

The 250F

The 250F Maserati was built from 1954 to 1958 and some have led a straightforward and uncomplicated life, their every move fully documented, while others have led a rough life, often starting in their early days when they were factory team cars. During the years 1954–56 the works cars and the customer cars became very mixed up and often confused. If the works team were short of a car, they would do a deal with an owner to borrow his car, put a works engine in it, respray it and take it to a race on paperwork for a factory car, changing the instrument panel identification and covering up the chassis number on the frame tube. They were even known to 'borrow' a customer's car without his knowledge. By 1956 the works-customer confusion reached an intolerable state, added to by the introduction of various experimental and test cars, so for 1957 the works team was kept completely separate from the customer department, with the result that Maserati had their most successful year and Fangio won the World Championship for them. At the end of 1957 the factory withdrew officially and gave more attention to customers, with the result that confusion returned.

2501   The production run had reached 2512 before this car appeared. It was part of the works team and was used throughout 1955–57 as a guinea pig for experimental work by the factory and led a very hard life. In 1958 the factory rebuilt it as new and gave it the identity 2526 and sold it to Keith Campbell, the Moto-Guzzi factory rider, who used it hardly at all. In later years it came to the UK.

*Stirling Moss retired his private 250F Maserati, chassis number 2508, in the 1954
International Trophy at Silverstone because of a broken de Dion tube.* (T. C. March)

2502   This was one of the first pair of cars that raced in the Argentine in
             January, 1954. Later that year it was raced as part of the factory
             team by Sergio Mantovani. It then disappeared either to be
             broken up or to be used as the basis for another car, or to repair a
             crashed car.

2503   Number never allocated to a 250F.

2504   Built in mid-1954 for Prince Birabongse to replace his interim
             car of the same number and using the engine from the earlier car.
             Raced by Bira until mid-1955. Sold to Horace Gould, then to
             Bruce Halford. Crashed by Halford and fitted with new chassis
             frame at the factory. Eventually went to New Zealand. Recently
             the remains were retrieved and resurrected as 2504. Now in a
             German collection.

2505   The car used by Fangio to win the model's first race in 1954.
             Used as part of the factory team. Later passed to André Simon
             and Joakim Bonnier. Lay fallow in Modena in 1958. Sub-
             sequently 'restored' by the factory and presented to the Biscaretti
             Museum in Turin as a typical 250F and given the identity 2500.

2506   Factory team car driven in 1954 by Marimon. Then sold to Louis
             Rosier and raced extensively by him. After spending many years
             in the Henri Malartre museum in Rochetillée-sur-Saône near
             Lyon, it passed to the Schlumpf Collection.

2507   This car was built to the order of Sid Greene and his Gilby
             Engineering Company. It was raced by Roy Salvadori in its first-
             line days and was a popular and regular competitor at many
             English circuits. During this time it was crashed at Oulton Park
             and went back to the factory to be rebuilt round a new chassis
             frame, retaining the number 2507. Before it was retired from
             racing Ivor Bueb drove it, and when it was no longer competitive
             it was 'retired' and sold to a private collector in Portugal. It
             remained in his care for many years until it returned to England
             to feature regularly in Historic racing.

2508   This car was ordered by the Moss family, through the Shell–BP
             company office in Italy. It was for Stirling Moss to compete in
             Grand Prix racing, as well as British National events. Before the

end of 1954 it had been taken into the Maserati works team, with Moss still as the driver, and special works engines were used in it. In 1955, when Moss joined the Mercedes-Benz team, he loaned the car to various drivers in order that it should continue to earn its keep. Among those who raced it were Bob Gerard, Mike Hawthorn, John Fitch and Lance Macklin. In a complicated financial deal it was sold to Ross Jensen in New Zealand and on paper changed its identity to 2513, but it did not change in fact, though it was put back to standard form. After many years in Australasia, it returned to England and then went to an American owner. It is still owned by Bob Sutherland, and bears its real identity 2508.

2509   This car was built to the order of the Owen Racing Organisation, the owners of B.R.M. They replaced any part that they knew had failed or broken on other 250F cars, and also made many modifications from their own racing experience, as well as trying out mechanical things that would be appearing on the new B.R.M. Ken Wharton, Peter Collins and Mike Hawthorn drove it. After the B.R.M. team had finished with it, it passed to Jack Brabham, and when it went out to New Zealand it was acquired by Chris Amon. It was still in its B.R.M.-modified form, and raced until no longer competitive, when it went into retirement in a museum. It still resides in Sir Len Southwood's museum in New Zealand and is in its B.R.M. condition. There is a 'built-up' car, numbered 2511, in the Schlumpf Museum with the old chassis frame from 2509. This is the original Owen Organization chassis, for the chassis of the Owen car, 2509, and Bira's car, 2504, were swapped after Ron Flockhart had crashed Bira's car while it was on loan to B.R.M.

2510   Number not allocated to a 250F. Paperwork sold with another chassis frame.

Monza, 1956: Jean Behra with the offset 250F, chassis number 2526, which retired because of a split fuel tank. (Publifoto)

In the 1957 Italian Grand Prix at Monza Juan Fangio (Maserati 250F) leads the Vanwalls of Moss, Brooks and Lewis Evans and the Maserati V-12 of Jean Behre. (Publifoto)

2511	Factory team car driven by Mantovani, then sold to Scuderia Centro-Sud and driven by a great variety of drivers. Retained by Centro-Sud long after they stopped racing and appears to have been totally dismantled over the years. Eventually the 'bones' were retrieved by Cameron Millar and resurrected into a new chassis frame 'Made in England' with new bodywork. Passed into the 'trade' and eventually ended up with a Japanese collector. The reconstructed car carries the identity of 2511. The 'composite' car in the Schlumpf Museum carries the same number.
2512	This is the car in which Marimon was killed at the Nürburgring in 1954. It was rebuilt and used by Mantovani as part of the factory team, and was last seen about mid-1955. All the evidence points to this being sold by the factory much later as 2518.
2513	The number 13 is not considered unlucky in Italy. The car was never completed by the factory, being sold to Tony Vandervell's Vanwall racing team for experimental purposes. It was complete with transaxle gearbox, suspension, brakes and so on, but without an engine or any bodywork. It stayed in the Vandervell factory at Park Royal after being used to investigate the 'state-of-the-art' of Formula 1 while the Vanwall Special was built. After Tony Vandervell's death, VP Products was acquired by GKN and eventually David Sankey, the son of one of the GKN directors, acquired the complete rolling chassis and had it completed with a built-up engine and a newly made body. In this form the car finally starting its racing career in VSCC Historic racing.
2514	This car was built in September, 1954, for Luigi Musso and in 1955 it was kept as part of the works team. Mantovani crashed it in practice at Turin in 1955, after which it was rebuilt by the works; at the end of the season it was sold to Horace Gould. He raced it in 1956–8 and then sold it to H. C. Spero. It was one of the first 250Fs to take part in Historic racing and raced regularly until it was sold to a Japanese collector.
2515	This was another factory team car built for 1955. Sold to the Scuderia Guastalla in 1956 and driven by Gerino Gerini, then sold to Ottorino Volonterio in 1957. He used it infrequently, but had it kept in 'as new' condition by the factory. Eventually he sold it to Tom Wheatcroft for the Donington Park Racing Car Museum.
2516	This was a 1956 factory team car that was subsequently sold to Reg Hunt in Australia. After a lot of racing 'down-under', it was brought to the UK by Cameron Millar, who kept it for many years as his 'favourite 250F'. Later sold to Anthony Mayman.
2517	Number never allocated, as in Italian sporting circles, and especially in card-playing gambling circles, 17 is considered to be very unlucky.
2518	This was a not-very-successful attempt at building an all-enveloping streamlined body on a normal 250F. After it was badly damaged in a fire at the works, the remains were stored, and the paperwork later sold with 2512, it would appear.
2519	This was built for Luigi Piotti, who raced it in 1956. In 1958 it was driven by Gerino Gerini in conjunction with the Scuderia Centro-Sud. Last seen at their factory around 1959–60.

In practice for the 1957 British Grand Prix at Aintree head mechanic Bertocchi discusses plugs with team leader Juan Fangio. (T. C. March)

Juan Fangio at the wheel of the lightweight 250F, chassis number 2528, in the 1957 British Grand Prix at Aintree. He retired because of engine problems. (T. C. March)

2520	A 1956 car for the factory team. It was subsequently sold to Stan Jones in Australia. Many years later, when 250Fs were fashionable in Historic racing, it came to the UK and was raced in VSCC events by David Llewellyn. Now owned by an Italian collector.
2521	Another 1956 factory team car, later sold to American John du Puy, living in Switzerland. Raced by Jean Lucas and André Testut, then sold to Serge Pozzoli who still owns it.
2522	A factory team car in 1956 that was sold to the Scuderia Centro-Sud in 1957. Used extensively by them to the end of their days. Parts of the car were retrieved by Cameron Millar and reconstructed on a new lightweight chassis frame 'Made in England'. Now with a Dutch collector.
2523(A)	This car is designated (A) as there were two cars on the factory books with the number 2523. In 1956, when the factory team was running short of cars and time, they cobbled up a car using the old bent chassis frame from 2507, which had been replaced by a new one. The damage was repaired and the car built as a team spare was given the number 2523, which was the point that the production run had reached. In August a new car took its place and number, so (A) less engine and vital parts was pushed into a corner. In 1957, when the first V-12 Maserati engine was ready to run, this old chassis was used as a test-bed and it was driven by all the team members during practice for various races. It was noted for the noise that came from the megaphone exhausts that ended on each side of the cockpit. When it was no longer needed for test purposes, the engine was removed and the car abandoned once again. In 1958 it was completely rebuilt by the factory to 'as new' condition with a 6-cylinder 250F engine and sold to Maria-Teresa de Filippis, who raced it in 1958. It then went to South America and in the 1970s came to the UK, less engine and one or two minor components, and is owned by Chris Drake.
2523(B)	This was built new in August 1956 as a spare car for the factory

Lightweight 'Piccolo' 250F, 2534, with Masten Gregory at the wheel in practice for the 1958 Italian Grand Prix at Monza. (Publifoto)

team to replace 2523(A). At the end of the year it went to the Australian Grand Prix with the factory team. Opinions vary as to whether it remained in Australia or returned to Italy and then went back to New Zealand as something else. In recent years a miscellaneous collection of parts purporting to be 2523(B) have been reconstructed into a whole and the car is in the USA.

2524   Built in 1956 for Francesco Godia-Sales of Spain. Sold to Joakim Bonnier in 1958 and later taken to the USA by him and sold to Phil Cade in 1961. Still owned by Cade.

2525   The first of a pair of special factory team cars with the engine angled to the left, allowing a lower seating position as the prop-shaft ran alongside the driver. New-style bodywork and fuel tank. It only raced in one event with the factory, the 1956 Italian Grand Prix. Then sold to Tony Parravano in California. After many years of inactivity it came to the UK and joined the JCB-Anthony Bamford collection. It then returned to the USA to join a private collection and was recently sold to another American collector.

2526   This was the second of the pair of cars specially built for the 1956 Italian Grand Prix. 2526 was not used again and remained at the factory until 1958, when it was refurbished and sold to Antonio Creus under the number 2530 (the number 2526 had already been applied to 2501 when sold to Keith Campbell). Creus only raced the car once before returning home to South America and it was subsequently sold to the Schlumpf brothers.

2527   The first of the most successful 1957 factory team cars, built on a tubular chassis frame similar to previous cars, but using much smaller-gauge tubing. This was known as the T2 chassis frame. The bodywork and shapely tail-tank followed the lines of the 'offset' car, number 2525. This car, and its two team-mates, soon became known as the 'Lightweight' cars, although it was only a relative term, compared to a new era of racing that was growing. In 1958 it was sold to Ken Kavannagh, the Australian Moto-Guzzi works rider, who was living in Italy. He had a few races with it, and it then lay fallow until it came to England to take part in VSCC Historic racing. During this time it had a very bad accident which necessitated the building of a virtually new chassis frame. It has been passed among VSCC 'racers' and collectors and is now in an American collection.

2528   The second of the factory team cars for 1957, with T2 chassis frame. In 1958 it was sold to Francesco Godia-Sales, and when it qualified for Historic racing it came to England. Owned by Neil Corner, it has been raced regularly and is one of Corner's favourite cars.

2529   The third of the 1957 factory team cars. This is the one that Fangio drove in the French Grand Prix at Rouen-les-Essarts, and the German Grand Prix at the Nürburgring, to establish himself as the ultimate master of the 250F Maserati, and to establish in some eyes the ultimate 250F. In 1958 it was brought from the factory by Giorgio Scarlatti, who raced it a few times and then sold it to Joakim Bonnier. He took it to the USA in 1959 and sold it to an American collector. It has been on display in the Cunningham Museum in California, but has now been sold to a German enthusiast.

2530   This was the first V-12-engined car to be built from scratch. It had a T2 'Lightweight' chassis frame and body panels and fuel tank-cum-tail like the three successful factory 6-cylinder cars of 1957. It first appeared at Rouen-les-Essarts for the 1957 French Grand Prix, and though driven in practice by Fangio, Schell and Menditeguy, it was not used in the race, and in fact was never seen again. The chassis number was transferred to 2526 when this was sold to Antonio Creus.

2531   This was the second V-12-engined car to be built from scratch. It had a 'Monza Offset'-type frame, like 2525 and 2526, with the engine mounted at an angle and the propshaft running diagonally across the cockpit to the left, allowing a lower seating position. It first appeared in practice at the Reims Grand Prix in 1957, but only survived a few laps in Behra's hands before a piston collapsed and ruined the engine. It next appeared at Pescara in 1957, again only used in practice, this time by Fangio and Behra, and then underwent quite a lot of development work. It actually raced in the Italian Grand Prix at Monza, driven by Jean Behra, but overheated and finally blew up. It appeared briefly for practice for the Modena Grand Prix and at Casablanca, and was never seen again. Less engine, it found its way to the Argentine and came to light recently, but was by no means complete, and certainly not with a 2½-litre V-12 engine in it.

2532   After chassis number 2529, it looked as though Maserati had built their last 6-cylinder Grand Prix car, especially when they closed down the racing department at the end of 1957, but early in 1958 the ex-V-12 car number 2530 was used to build an experimental 6-cylinder car. It was completed and out on test at the Nürburgring early in the season, complete with a late-development 6-cylinder engine, and then it appeared briefly in practice for the Belgian Grand Prix, looked after by factory personnel, who were very non-committal about its reason and destination. The identity plate 2532 appeared on a car at Reims in 1958, driven by Fangio in his last race, but subsequently it turned out that this car was *not* 2532. The experimental car built on the T2 'Lightweight' frame of 2530 that had been seen at the Nürburgring and Spa eventually found its way to the Argentine, and in recent years some of the parts came back to England. The car was resurrected with a new English-built chasis frame, and many other new parts, and reappeared as 2532, but it must be said that the real remains of 2532 are still in South America, and could one day come to the surface.

2533   Eventually, during the 1958 season, the reason for the mysterious experimental car 2532 became apparent. An American named Temple Buell was financing his own private Scuderia and Maserati built him two brand-new cars. These were on T3 super-lightweight or 'Piccolo' chassis frames with shorter wheelbases, lighter and smaller, with the drive-shafts angled slightly forwards. 2533 was the first of these. After a trip to New Zealand in company with two other Maseratis, as the Scuderia El Salvador, this car returned to the factory and in 1961 was sold to Joe Lubin in America. He kept the car until 1984, when it was bought by Don Orosco, who had it completely overhauled and raced it at Silverstone in 1986.

2534   This was the second of the Temple Buell 'Piccolo' cars and was completed in September 1958. After residing in an Italian collection for many years it came to England in 1972 and joined the Bamford Collection and has enlivened VSCC and Historic racing driven by Willie Green.

'Tec-Mec'   This project was begun in the Maserati factory, but was not completed when the racing department closed down. It was a logical development of the 'Piccolo' cars, begun by Valerio Colotti. When Maserati turned its activities to production GT cars, Colotti left the firm and set up his own design-studio in the town of Modena, forming Officine Tecnica Meccanica. After many problems this special one-off project, now called Tec-Mec, was completed, using an old 6-cylinder 250F engine, and the car made one brief appearance in the American Grand Prix. It eventually ended up in the Donington Racing Car Museum. Had it been given a Maserati chassis number, it would have been 2535.

It is necessary to mention briefly eight more 250Fs that never saw the workshop floor of the Maserati factory. These have been wholly or partly built by Cameron Millar and all are stamped with his CM serial number. Although they are totally acceptable to the Vintage Sports Car Club under its special category, Group 4, they have no place in this book.

Mercedes-Benz

Both Daimler, with Mercedes cars, and Benz were into racing at an early stage of the sport and industry, and Gottlieb Daimler built a special competition car, the Canstatt-Daimler, as early as 1899. Carl Benz toyed with racing cars in a relatively small way, but Daimler's Mercedes racing cars were numerous, and mostly successful. The 1914 Mercedes Grand Prix cars set trends and standards that ruled for many years.

In the early vintage years there were racing Mercedes with 4-cylinder and 8-cylinder engines; the 2-litre 8-cylinder of 1924 was very fast, but rather tricky to handle. When Daimler and Benz joined forces in 1926 to form Daimler-Benz and make Mercedes-Benz cars, they concentrated on sports-car racing, rather than Grand Prix racing. That was until the Third Reich and financial inducement was offered to German companies prepared to tackle the new Grand Prix Formula in 1934, and promote 'Deutschland über alles'.

Daimler-Benz started a technical programme on the strength of government subsidies and military contracts that saw Grand Prix racing rise to phenomenal heights, a technical standard that has only recently been surpassed in Formula 1. It all began with the W25, built in 1934 and developed through 1935 and 1936 to culminate in 1937 with the W125, which was an absolute peak in front-engined Grand Prix cars. This line of Mercedes-Benz single-seater cars was based on a very light and strong tubular chassis frame with independent suspension to all four wheels, hydraulic brakes (a very advanced feature for the time), and a straight-eight, twin-cam, 32-valve engine with sophisticated supercharging and special fuel. The rear suspension of the W25 was on the swing-axle principle that had

The 1924 2-litre Mercedes 8-cylinder car, seen here with Raymond Mays at the wheel at Brooklands. (The Geoffrey Goddard Collection)

The 1935 Mercedes-Benz W25 driven here by Louis Chiron in the French Grand Prix at Montlhéry. (The Geoffrey Goddard Collection)

roadholding limitations, and in 1937 the W125 development used a de Dion rear suspension sprung on torsion bars; the front suspension used double wishbones and coil springs.

The supercharged 5.6-litre straight-eight engine of the W125 was undoubtedly the most powerful Grand Prix engine of the pre-war years, and its bhp output was not surpassed until recent times, when 1500 cc turbo-charged engines came on the Grand Prix scene.

In 1938 a new Formula came into being, limiting engine capacity to 3 litres, if supercharged, and Daimler-Benz built four-camshaft V-12 engines and used a direct development of the W125 chassis with its de Dion rear suspension. This was the W154, and in 1939 it became the W154/163, using the M163 engine, which was a two-stage supercharger version of the V-12. In terms of circuit potential, which combines engine power with handling, road-holding and braking, the W154/163 was higher than the W125, and represents the peak of Grand Prix car development of the pre-war period.

After a brief foray in South America in 1951 with their 1939 cars, Daimler-Benz prepared to tackle Grand Prix racing again with the introduction of a new Formula

The 1937 straight-eight 5.6-litre Mercedes-Benz W125. (The Author's Collection)

The V-12 Mercedes-Benz 3-litre M154 engine in 1938 single-stage supercharged form.
(The Author's Collection)

In 1939 Mercedes-Benz raced the 3-litre W154 with two-stage supercharged M163 engine.
(The Author's Collection)

in 1954, which limited engines to 2500 cc without superchargers, or 750 cc with supercharger. Daimler-Benz went the unblown route, like everyone else, and their W196 Grand Prix cars simply bristled with innovations. The twin-cam straight-eight engine was lying on its side, the valve gear was fully mechanical (desmodromic) without valve springs, direct fuel injection into the cylinders was used, the chassis was a multi-tube space-frame of perfect conception, suspension was independent on all four wheels, enormous drum brakes were mounted inboard on the sprung part of the chassis, the front ones driven by shafts from the

Juan Fangio at the wheel of the streamlined Mercedes-Benz W196 on the model's winning debut at Reims in 1954. (LAT)

front hubs, the 5-speed gearbox was behind the rear axle and the bodywork was fully streamlined and all-enveloping.

The W196 appeared mid-way through the 1954 season and won its first race at Reims. It then set the pace for Grand Prix racing in face of opposition from Ferrari, Maserati, Gordini, B.R.M., Vanwall and Lancia. Various versions of the W196 were built, with differing wheelbase lengths and differing body styles, and it was a case of individual specifications for each circuit. By mid-1955, a year after the first appearance, the Mercedes-Benz team had a stranglehold on Grand Prix racing, as evidenced by finishing 1-2-3-4 in the British Grand Prix.

At the end of 1955 the Daimler-Benz management withdrew the Mercedes-Benz team from Grand Prix racing. Official demonstrations have been frequently made with a W196, and with earlier models, but no further Grand Prix race entries have ever been made. That the Research & Development Department of Daimler-Benz have not lost touch with high speed was evidenced a few years ago when a Mercedes-Benz turbocharged single-seater record car lapped the Fiat-Nardo test track in southern Italy to take records at over 250 mph.

Throughout the activity of the Mercedes-Benz racing cars since 1934 the firm never sold any of their cars, though they loaned some to museums, and actually gave some to favoured museums, but they were not in working order and some had even had vital parts removed! During the 1939–45 war the 1939 cars were dispersed throughout Eastern Europe for safe keeping from British bombing attacks. After the war Daimler-Benz did not get them all back.

One from Czechoslovakia was sold to the USA, via England, in 1946; another from Romania was sold to the USA in 1971, and a W125 escaped through Berlin to England in 1968. All three have been made to run over the years, the Czech car having a bad time at Indianapolis in 1947, 1948, and through to 1951. The 5.6-litre was made to run well enough to take part in small Historic races. Eventually the car that ran at Indianapolis came to England and has now been totally rebuilt, and the Romanian car has also been rebuilt in England for a new American owner. After its brief outings in Historic events the 5.6-litre W125 was sold to a Japanese collector.

The Daimler-Benz museum has kept two of the 1939 cars, as well as a 1935 and a 1937 car, and have loaned a 1937 and a 1939 car to the Schlumpf Museum in France. Another W125 is in the Deutsches Museum in Munich.

A second car that was in Czechoslovakia came to the Donington Park Museum for a time, but is now back in the Prague Museum, and the second car in Rumania was crashed many years ago and languishes in a derelict state. There were two cars dispersed to Poland, but only one has surfaced, in incomplete form, in the Schlumpf Museum.

In addition to all their pre-war Grand Prix activities Daimler–Benz found time to build two mini-Grand Prix cars of 1500 cc especially to take part in, and win, the 1939 Tripoli Grand Prix, which the Italians restricted to 1500 cc in an effort to keep the Germans out. These supercharged V-8-engined cars were scaled-down versions of the W154/163 Grand Prix cars. They only ran in that one race, and gave one demonstration run on the Nürburgring. During the war they were hidden away in Switzerland and returned to Stuttgart in later years, where they are still retained.

Miller–Ford V-8

Getting the Ford Motor Company involved in Indianapolis racing in 1935 was the work of entrepreneur Preston Tucker, who talked Edsel Ford into financing a team of cars for the 1935 race. Tucker joined forces with Harry Miller to produce the cars, and the trade and industry assumed they would be Ford-orientated cars, the original scheme being to use 'stock' Ford components and thus reap the benefit of success in enhanced sales. As things turned out the only Ford components used were the engines, and these were the rather unlikely 3.6-litre side-valve V-8s, which had recently been introduced. The car itself was a classic example of Harry Miller's work, with front-wheel drive, all-independent suspension, very low centre of gravity and a very sleek regulation two-seater body set off by a radiator grille like those used on the production Ford V-8 and the V-8 symbol on the side.

There was nothing wrong with Miller's car, and its cornering speeds on the Indianapolis track were more than adequate, but the side-valve Ford V-8 engine, even with special alloy cylinder heads, high compression ratio and multiple carburettors, was totally inadequate; a mere 150 bhp being quoted, so the cars were not in the top class. Ten cars were built, but only four of them qualified for the race, the others being too slow, and the result was total failure. All four failed to finish. **159**

Ted Horn at Indianapolis in 1935 with his front-wheel-drive Miller-Ford V-8. (The Geoffrey Goddard Collection)

Under-bonnet heat caused the steering boxes to expand and seize the mechanism on three of the cars, and the fourth suffered similar heat expansion of its front-drive unit.

Henry Ford had been against the whole project from the start and after the race he ordered that all the cars should be impounded and locked away in one of his factories. There they stayed until 1937, when they were discreetly disposed of to suitable people. They did not reappear as Ford V-8 racing cars, but the Miller parts were utilized in the building of other Indianapolis cars, some of which proved quite successful. Two seem to have survived in original form, one in the Ford Museum at Dearborn and the other in a private collection.

Multi-Union

By definition the Multi-Union could be described as a special, but that would not do it justice, for in concept and execution it could have come from the best racing car factory or industry research and development department. It was constructed by J. S. Worters, a motorcycle tuner of long standing at the Brooklands track, but he was ably assisted by some of the best brains and facilities in the motor industry.

The whole idea of the car came from Chris Staniland, who was chief test pilot for Fairey Aviation and an accomplished racing driver able to compete with the best in anything from hill-climbs to record-breaking. He had been racing a 1934 Alfa Romeo Tipo B (Chassis 5003, *see* Tipo B entry) and felt that it could provide the basis of a very competitive special. Through his aircraft contacts he enlisted the help of the Lockheed brake company and High Duty Alloys, who in turn had good contacts with Rolls-Royce at Derby.

The main drawback on the Tipo B Alfa Romeo was its 3-speed gearbox, so the first thing that was done was to design and manufacture a new gearbox with four speeds. Another Tipo B limitation was the rod-operated braking system, so this was replaced with a Lockheed hydraulic system and that firm also made bigger and better brake drums and better internal components, while the very latest two-leading-shoe Lockheed system was used. Worters stiffened the Alfa Romeo chassis frame, modified the leaf spring suspension and strengthened the twin-propshaft final drive. Wherever possible components were lowered, to cut down frontal area, and a very smooth wind-cheating body was made in aluminium.

The straight-eight 2.9-litre Alfa Romeo engine, with its twin superchargers, was administered to and the car was ready for racing in the spring of 1938. In was given the intriguing name of Multi-Union, a typically English play on words aping the famous German Auto Union. It created quite a stir on the British racing scene and before the end of the 1938 season it had won the Phoenix Park race in Ireland at an average of 97.45 mph and took the Brooklands Outer Circuit record for 3-litre cars at 141.45 mph, adding more than 11 mph to the old record. At that time only two other cars had lapped Brooklands at over 140 mph, the Barnato-Hassan with its 8-litre Bentley engine, and the Napier-Railton with its 24-litre Napier Lion engine. Staniland also set new International 3-litre records for 5 km (139.5 mph), 5 miles (139.9 mph), 10 km (139.6 mph) and 10 miles (138.9 mph) using the 2¾-mile banked track.

Chris Staniland with the Multi-Union II on the Campbell Circuit at Brooklands in August, 1939. (The Geoffrey Goddard Collection)

With this first-season success a major redesign took place the following winter, resulting in Multi-Union II. The front of the Alfa Romeo chassis was cut off and the rigid-beam Alfa axle was replaced by an Italian Tecnauto independent system which used trailing link geometry and springing by twisting square-section coil springs. The Alfa rear suspension was removed and the twin-propshaft rear axle was sprung on exposed coil springs and located by tubular rods. Lockheed came up with even bigger and better hydraulic brakes, and the supercharging arrangements were improved with new casings and longer rotors and a revised inlet manifolding. The oil tank was removed from the tail and replaced by one on the left of the cockpit and the body was reprofiled and lowered. There were many details that clearly stemmed from the aircraft industry, such as the shallow vee radiator, hydraulic control of the throttles and remote control of the various filler caps, concealed under flush-fitting flaps in the bodywork.

Unfortunately all this took longer than anticipated, added to which increased activity in experimental aircraft for the RAF kept Staniland very busy in the air. The Multi-Union II was entered for the August Brooklands meeting, which eventually turned out to be the last ever, and it ran in a Campbell road-circuit race and an Outer Circuit handicap. During the latter the engine went on to seven cylinders, due to internal trouble, but none the less put in a lap at 142.3 mph. It was scheduled to have made an attack on the out-and-out lap record, which stood at 143.44 mph, but the engine trouble was terminal so the record attempt was abandoned. There is little doubt that it would have set a new record, but war was to prevent any further activity.

Chris Staniland, the only man to have raced the Multi-Union, was killed while test-flying during the war and this most interesting special was never to be seen performing in its 1939 manner again.

Since 1946 it has languished about in various workshops, making a few desultory appearances in VSCC racing, but it has been a shadow of its true self, though little has been changed apart from rebuilding the engine with new cylinder blocks to replace the original damaged ones. Today it is with VSCC Alfa Romeo owners. If we had a Ministry of Motor Racing looking after our heritage the Multi-Union II would have been mounted on a plinth in a museum long ago, as a superb example of British enterprise and craftsmanship of the immediate pre-1939 war period, and as a memorial to Flt. Lt. C. S. Staniland, one of the test pilots who helped to make the Royal Air Force the strong military arm that it was. 'Genuine.'

Napier-Railton

This famous car has a distinction that can never be taken away from it. It is the fastest car that has ever lapped the defunct Brooklands banked track, an achievement it recorded in 1935 when it was driven by its owner John Cobb, at an average speed of 143.44 mph. Right through to the last Brooklands meeting in August 1939 others were trying to take the record from the Napier-Railton, and some came mighty close, but the imposing great car was never beaten.

It was built in 1933 by Thomson & Taylor the racing engineers in their works within the Weybridge track, to the order of John Cobb, a London businessman whose hobby was motor racing. Cobb had a number of objectives in view when he commissioned the car, foremost being Outer Circuit racing at Brooklands, with the lap record as an obvious aim, and also long-distance World and International records. Power was to be provided by a 'broad-arrow' 12-cylinder Napier Lion aero engine of 24 litres, capable of giving an easy and reliable 500 bhp. The brilliant young designer Reid Railton set to work on the chassis and T&T virtually carved everything from the solid. A massive underslung girder chassis frame was built, housing the 12-cylinder Napier engine in the front, coupled to a simple 3-speed gearbox with an open propeller shaft running back to the specially made E.N.V. rear axle. Semi-elliptic leaf springs were used at the front, mounted under the massive axle beam, and at the rear there were two long cantilever leaf springs on each side of the frame. The driving seat was to the right of the propeller shaft

John Cobb with the 24-litre Napier-Railton at Brooklands in 1934. (The Geoffrey Goddard Collection)

and a 15-gallon oil tank sat between the shaft and the near-side frame member. A 65-gallon fuel tank filled the tail. The bodywork was simple and functional, there being little need to worry about streamlining as the Napier Lion produced far more power than was really needed, but it meant that it would run reliably for long periods without undue stress. No front brakes were fitted, as the car was designed for track racing and record runs in which rear brakes would suffice.

It was finished in a silver grey with black wheels and was ready by mid-season. From then until the end of 1937, when Cobb pensioned it off to concentrate on a new project, it spent its whole life at speeds of over 120 mph, and a lot of the time at over 130 mph, and not a few miles at over 140 mph. It recorded the highest speed ever at the Brooklands track when it was timed at 151.97 mph over the flying kilometre. In 1935 it won the 500-mile race at 121.28 mph and in 1937 it won the fastest-ever race at the Surrey track when it averaged 136.03 mph in the 10-lap Broadcast Trophy. At the end of 1937 it won the 500-kilometre race at 127.05 mph and thus ended its Brooklands career, during which it had broken the one-lap record no fewer than four times, at 137.20 mph, 139.71 mph, 140.93 mph and 143.44 mph.

Apart from its Brooklands track exploits the Napier-Railton left its mark on the field of record-breaking, Cobb taking it to the Montlhéry Track in France, and to the Bonneville Salt flats at Utah in the United States. At Montlhéry it set new records in 1933 and 1934 from 200 miles to 2000 miles, the former at 126.84 mph and the latter at 120.71 mph. In 1935 and 1936 Cobb took the great car to Utah and set records from 1 hour to 24 hours, his greatest achievement being to take the World Hour record at 167.69 mph in 1936, and the 24-hour record at 150.6 mph. Not many cars have travelled so far and so fast in a short span of four years. For these long-distance record runs Cobb was assisted by 'Tim' Rose-Richards, Charlie Dodson, John Hindmarsh and Charles Brackenbury, while his earlier Montlhéry record runs were driven with the assistance of Charles Brackenbury, Cyril Paul and Freddie Dixon. For the long-distance Brooklands races he was aided by Oliver Bertram and Rose-Richards.

The size and strength of the Napier-Railton made it a true giant among racing cars and its success and reliability were characteristic of Thomson & Taylor and Reid Railton. It was not used during 1938 and 1939, and was then carefully stored for the war years, but the changing scene after the war meant that it never ran again in the manner for which it had been built.

John Cobb lost his life after the war while making an attempt on the Water Speed record, but before this he had hired the Napier-Railton to a film company to make *Pandora and the Flying Dutchman*, in which the car had to represent a 400 mph record-car, which it did admirably, thinly disguised with altered body-work, which included a sort of bird-cage out in front of the radiator, a long tapering tail and a head fairing behind the cockpit.

After Cobb's death the car lay dormant, and might well have been broken up had not Sir Geoffrey Quilter of the G.Q. Parachute Company had the brilliant idea of acquiring it to use for testing arrester parachutes for bombers. The old car, weighing 1½ tons, was quite happy to gallop up to 140 mph on an airfield runway and be slowed by a parachute emerging from a structure mounted above the tail, though huge disc brakes replaced the primitive drum brakes as a safety measure.

This episode in its life came to an end when Sir Geoffrey Quilter died and it seemed as though it might be the end of the Napier-Railton. But it was not, for the Hon. Patrick Lindsay acquired it and audaciously ran it in Historic races at Silverstone and Oulton Park. It later passed into the hands of Bob Roberts, who had it completely restored and put back into its Brooklands form, and it holds pride of place in his Midlands Motor Museum, making occasional sorties for 'demonstration' purposes, but it must feel very frustrated at not being allowed to stretch its legs into its normal gait of anywhere between 130 and 170 mph, where it spent most of its active life.

'Genuine '

Acknowledgements to Profile Publications Number 28 by William Boddy; *The History of Brooklands Motor Course* by William Boddy; and Brooklands Parade Number 19, *The Motor*, 23 September, 1942.

O.B.M.

Oscar Moore at the wheel of the B.M.W.-powered O.B.M. at Prescott in June, 1948. (Guy Griffiths)

The O.B.M. was built by Oscar B. Moore, a North London motor trader operating under the name of Purkess Ltd in Finchley. He had long been a sporting and competition motorist, and after the 1939–45 war he was soon in action with a 1937 Frazer Nash-B.M.W. Type 328, registered GHX 516. With the advent of Formula 2 for International racing in 1948, Moore removed the body from his 328, moved the driving position in towards the centre of the car and made himself a 'quasi' single-seater with a contemporary-styled bodywork, with a cowled radiator and head fairing behind the cockpit.

Magnesium-alloy wheels were fitted to reduce the unsprung weight, and the engine was tuned to run on methanol, with higher compression ratio, etc. For not a great deal of expenditure Moore had himself a 130 mph 2-litre Formula 2 car with which he could compete in all the European races.

The car was finished in 1948 and had a very active 1949 season, affording its owner much pleasure but little in the way of success, as it could not match purpose-built Formula 2 cars. With the end of Formula 2 in 1953 the car was sold and passed into the Club racing world and gradually disappeared into limbo, though it still exists, owned by an amateur enthusiast, but has not been seen for many years.

'Genuine '

Osca

When the Maserati brothers left the firm in Modena in 1947 they returned to Bologna, where they had started Automobile Maserati in 1926, and started a new firm under the name of Officine Specializate Construzione Automobili, which gave them the name Osca. Racing was still very much in their blood and they concentrated on competition cars, building superb little racing/sports cars of 1100 cc and 1500 cc, but they never lost their interest in pure single-seater racing cars.

'B. Bira' (Prince Birabongse) with his 4½-litre V-12 Osca-powered Maserati 4CLT/48 in the Formule Libre race at Silverstone in July, 1952. (T. C. March)

Chiron's 2-litre Osca at the 1953 Italian Grand Prix. Behind the car Chiron is in conversation with Louis Rosier. (LAT)

Amédée Gordini was working in a similar vein in Paris, and he designed a Formula 1 engine, a very compact V-12 unit of 4½ litres capacity, but then could not raise the finance to produce it. The Maserati brothers did a deal with him and took over the design and modified it to fit into the current Maserati 4CLT/48 chassis frame. This was a good move because the 16-valve 4-cylinder Maserati engine dated back to 1939 and had reached the end of its life for use in front-line Grand Prix racing. Unfortunately this new engine took longer to produce than anticipated, and by the time it was running and delivering 300 bhp, at least another 100 bhp was needed to be competitive with the Ferrari and Alfa Romeo opposition. Added to this, the Maserati chassis was getting obsolete, with its non-independent rear axle, so the V-12 Osca project did not take off.

One engine was sold to 'B. Bira', who already had a 4CLT/48 Maserati, and it was slotted into the Maserati chassis in place of the supercharged 1½-litre 4-cylinder engine. It did not appear until the 1951 season, by which time the Formula was reaching the end of its life. Although Bira had a few races with the V-12 Osca-Maserati he achieved little, which was a pity, for had it been available two years earlier it might have been very competitive. Towards the end of 1951, with only two races left to run, a brand new V-12 Osca appeared for the Italian GP at Monza, driven by Franco Rol. This was a car built in its entirety at the Bologna factory, with tubular steel chassis, double-wishbone and coil spring I.F.S. and de Dion rear suspension.

In 1952 Grand Prix racing was demoted to 2-litre Formula 2 and Osca built two neat little F2 cars, both powered by a 6-cylinder version of their racing/sports car 4-cylinder 1500 cc engine, a straightforward twin overhead camshaft design. The chassis was a scaled-down version of the singleton Formula 1 Osca and they were raced by Elie Bayol and Louis Chiron until the Grand Prix Formula changed yet again in 1954. With the introduction of Formula Junior towards the end of the 1950s a pretty little Osca Junior was built, but it never went into production.

The V-12 Maserati-Osca led a fairly active but chequered career, being sold to Australia, where it was 'raced into the ground'. It then transferred to England to make sporadic appearances in Historic racing, and was finally rebuilt and put back to the 1951 condition and joined the moribund old Grand Prix cars in the Donington Racing Car Museum. The V-12 Osca lives in a French collection, while the Elie Bayol F2 car was brought into England and made a few appearances in Historic racing. The Chiron F2 cars remained in France in the collector/museum world.

R.R.A.

Motor racing enthusiast and garage owner Geoff Richardson was among the first to become part of the national racing scene after the war. He acquired the Percy Maclure E.R.A.-engined racing Riley in 1948 and over the next few years he rebuilt it into a special of his own conception. Taking a leaf from English Racing Automobiles (E.R.A.) and British Racing Motors (B.R.M.), Geoff Richardson came up with Richardson Racing Automobiles (R.R.A.).

The car had started life as a racing Riley, around 1935, and Percy Maclure had developed it into a Riley Special over the years, ending up with André-Girling I.F.S. and an E.R.A. power unit installed. Richardson continued the development and by the time he had finished very little was left of the original Riley, and

Geoff Richardson with his E.R.A.-powered R.R.A. Special at Castle Combe in October, 1950. (Guy Griffiths)

even the 1½-litre E.R.A. engine had been enlarged to 2 litres. It was no longer a low, offset driving position, single-seater; a new chassis frame replaced the Riley one and the driver sat centrally. The André Girling independent front suspension was retained, but the Riley rear axle was replaced by a swing-axle independent layout. A completely new body was made, which changed the whole outward character of the car.

Eventually this R.R.A. went the way of all specials, being dismantled to form the basis of yet another special. The second R.R.A. began with an Aston Martin DB3S chassis frame replacing the Rubery Owen frame of the first R.R.A. and the E.R.A. engine was replaced by a 3.4-litre Jaguar power unit, so the 2-litre E.R.A. engine was sold to another special builder. The R.R.A.-Jaguar was raced for a season and then made way for a third R.R.A., which was more contemporary, consisting of a rear-engined Formula 1 Cooper with the Coventry Climax engine replaced by a 2½-litre Connaught/Alta engine.

The R.R.A.-Jaguar was made into a road-going sports car after Geoff pensioned it off, and his third R.R.A. was also sold when he gave up racing and turned to aircraft as his hobby. Even the Cooper-Connaught changed character almost immediately, for the 4-cylinder engine was replaced by a V-8 Buick engine.

Geoff Richardson's B.R.A. cars came, performed and disappeared, but in recent years a 'Facsimile' of the original Riley-E.R.A. has been built by a friend of Geoff Richardson, and Geoff himself has assisted greatly in this 're-creation' of the car that started Richardson Racing Automobiles.

Riley

It was not until the advent of the 4-cylinder ohv Riley Nine engine in 1926 that the name of the famous Coventry firm began to become closely associated with motor racing. The little 1100 cc engine, with its inclined overhead valves operated by two camshafts mounted high in the iron cylinder block and operating the valves by short pushrods and rockers, was an inspired design. It became the basis of the low-slung 'Brooklands Model' sports car, which in turn became the basis for numerous Riley Nine 'Specials'.

While the Riley firm continued to develop sports/racing versions, the pure single-seater scene was left to the amateur tuner and specialists such as Freddie Dixon and Frank Ashby. The fastest 1100 cc Riley was undoubtedly Dixon's 'Red Mongrel' single-seater, which lapped the Brooklands track at 113 mph.

Using the same inclined-valve hemispherical combustion chamber layout, Riley developed a new 1½-litre 6-cylinder version, and enlarged the 4-cylinder to 1½ litres. The name Riley was kept in the forefront of racing and record breaking by George Eyston, Edgar Maclure, Hector Dobbs and others. Most of the development work was with multiple carburettors rather than supercharging, and Dixon's 2-litre Riley Special with six SU carburettors was immensely fast, capable of well over 130 mph. He also did a lot of development work on all the other parts of the car, reducing weight, improving streamlining, changing the weight distribution, stiffening the chassis and improving the brakes and suspension. Dixon's two special Rileys were the high-point in racing Rileys, and both are still in existence today, though they are not often seen.

In 1936 the Riley company offered for sale a single-seater of their own, with

Fred Dixon with his 2-litre Riley at Brooklands in the mid-thirties (The Geoffrey Goddard Collection)

The Riley Maclure Special driven by Sheila Darbyshire at Prescott in May, 1947. (Guy Griffiths)

Mrs. Elsie Wisdom with the factory I.F.S. Riley 4-cylinder single-seater in the International Trophy race at Brooklands in 1936. (R. H. Fuller)

independent front suspension by the André Girling system of swing axles and coil springs, but it was not a great success. However, Edgar Maclure's young brother, Percy, had been developing his own racing 1100 cc Riley and in typical special-building manner the original car was being changed continuously. By 1938 the Maclure Riley had taken over where Dixon had left off, and it incorporated the factory I.F.S.

In 1933 Raymond Mays had instigated a development programme on a 6-cylinder 1½-litre Riley which ultimately sired the E.R.A., and the 'guinea pig' supercharged Riley/E.R.A. engine from the Mays car by 1939 had found its way into the Maclure Riley. After the war this Riley Special was very active until it became absorbed into Geoff Richardson's R.R.A. as described elsewhere.

The sound but uncomplicated Riley ohv design has always been popular with amateur tuners and special builders, and though the firm did not build many pure racing single-seaters, their sports/racing car development programme was extensive and involved a lot of special racing components that could be used in a single-seater. Even today Riley Specials are being assembled by enthusiasts from production components and the Riley movement forms the backbone of the lower-income section of the VSCC.

Rolland-Pilain

The French Rolland-Pilain firm dates back to 1906 as the makers of quality touring cars, but after the First World War they got carried away with enthusiasm for Grand Prix racing, as did many other French manufacturers. They built a team of cars for the 1922 French Grand Prix at Strasbourg, and though they were technically interesting they were not very successful. They were built in the Rolland-Pilain factory in Tours and had straight-eight 2-litre engines, with twin overhead camshafts, using four carburettors.

The chassis was well proportioned with a narrower rear track than that at the

The remaining Rolland-Pilain Grand Prix car of the Rochetailleé-sur-Sâone Museum. (The Author)

front, and in line with current thinking the cockpit was of two-seater width. Unusual, however, was the positioning of the driver on the left, in compliance with normal French road driving as distinct from racing, where most road-circuits were run clockwise and most racing cars were built with right-hand steering.

The racing life of the Rolland-Pilain team was very short, though they did manage to win the 1923 San Sebastian Grand Prix. Two of the cars were later fitted with 6-cylinder cuff-valve Schmid engines, and ran under the name Schmid. The third car remained unaltered and is still in existence today, living in retirement in Henri Malartre's Museum at Rochetaillée-sur-Saône in France.

Rover

The idea of a racing 'Auntie' Rover seems very incongruous, but that is what happened in 1948. It was not an official Rover factory project, though it had close connections, as the progenitors were young Rover engineers who built it in their spare time.

Rover had introduced their new post-war P4 design, with 6-cylinder overhead inlet, side exhaust engine in a very robust chassis with wishbone and coil spring independent front suspension. The three young engineers, Spencer King, Peter Wilks and George Mackay, created their single-seater from production components, reducing the engine capacity to 1996 cc so that the car qualified for the new Formula 2 category. Production I.F.S. was used, but a de Dion layout was designed for the rear, the principles of which eventually passed back into the Rover experimental department.

The designers ran it in short circuit racing and in hill-climbs during 1949 and 1950, and when the company directors gave it their blessing it was used for some experimental work on suspension and roadholding for the benefit of the firm.

Having served its purpose it was sold to vintage racing enthusiast Frank Lockhart, who has raced it ever since, it still being in continual use after nearly 40 years.

P. M. Wilks with the single-seater Rover at Prescott hill climb in June, 1949.
(Guy Griffiths)

For a long period of its 'Historic' career it was fitted with a 3-litre Rover engine, a development assisted by its creators. They took enormous pleasure from 'dicing' the car round the Rover test-track, even though they had reached the position of 'top executives' within the Rover firm.

Today it is back to its Formula 2 form, with 2-litre engine, but still goes surprisingly well for an 'Auntie' Rover.

S.E.F.A.C.

In 1930 a company was formed in France known as *Societé des Études et de Fabrication d'Automobile de Course*, which, as its name implied, was for the study and building of racing cars. It was not a very successful firm, for they only built one racing car, and that has gone down in history as one of the biggest flops of all time. Using the initials of the firm the car was called the the S.E.F.A.C. and it had been designed by Émile Petit, who had designed the successful Salmson cars in the 1920s.

The object was to provide a French challenger for Grand Prix honours in the 1934–37 period of racing to the 750 kilogram weight limit formula. It was 1935 before the S.E.F.A.C. arrived in public, when it practised for the French Grand Prix. Compared to the new German cars it was hopeless, and was withdrawn from the event.

The only thing you could say about the S.E.F.A.C. was that it was different. The Petit-designed engine was probably all right in theory, but was not very good in practical terms. There were two 4-cylinder blocks mounted side by side on a single crankcase, each block having a cylinder head with twin overhead camshafts. In the crankcase were two crankshafts mounted side by side and geared together, so that they ran in opposite directions. The right-hand crank drove a large supercharger from its rear end, and the left-hand crank drove the gearbox, so that the propeller shaft ran down the left side of the wide chassis frame. This allowed the driver to sit low, alongside, but made for a wide car. The channel-section steel

The 8-cylinder S.E.F.A.C. seen at the 1935 French Grand Prix with Marcel Lehoux at the wheel. (The Geoffrey Goddard Collection)

chassis frame carried independent front suspension and a rigid rear axle, coil springs being used at all four corners. The whole car was far too heavy and the engine was cumbersome, compared to a straight-eight, while the bodywork made the S.E.F.A.C. one of the ugliest cars to grace the Grand Prix scene.

After many promises it failed to appear again and the firm became moribund, but in 1938 there was a resurgence of interest. A new Grand Prix Formula had been announced, limiting supercharged engines to 3 litres, with no maximum weight limit for the car. Émile Petit produced his car once more, as its 2.8-litre engine was eligible and its weight was unimportant. It was marginally more successful than in 1935 in that it actually started in the 1938 French Grand Prix, though it retired almost instantly. It made one more appearance, in 1939 in the Pau Grand Prix, and that was it, the S.E.F.A.C. disappeared for ever more. As one British racing driver at the time said, 'I went to see the S.E.F.A.C., and could SEFAC-ALL'.

In 1948 the French motoring press announced a new French contender for Grand Prix honours, from the firm Dommartin. It was none other than Émile Petit and his S.E.F.A.C., now devoid of its supercharger to comply with the new rules, and enlarged to 3.6 litres. It never appeared in public.

There has never been a sign of this strange racing car since, but that does not mean that it could never reappear. One day someone is going to find an old racing car in the cellars of a long-forgotten French château and it is going to turn out to be the S.E.F.A.C.

Scarab

The Scarab cars were built by Reventlow Automobiles Inc. a firm created by young Lance Reventlow, heir to the Woolworth fortunes. When he started sports car racing in the United States, he was not content to buy a 'foreign' car like most of his contemporaries. He gathered a strong force of sound people together and formed his own company to build sports/racing cars using American engines and gearboxes, and these were very successful in American domestic racing in 1957. One of his aims was to take part in Grand Prix racing, patriotically carrying the Stars and Stripes.

Had the Scarab Formula 1 cars appeared in 1957, or even in 1958, they might have been successful, but the project was a bit too ambitious for the facilities and took too long to complete. It was 1960 before they appeared in Europe and by then the 'rear-engine revolution' was in full spate, with races and circuits being tailored for the nimble little Cooper and Lotus cars.

The Scarab was extremely well made, with a sound space-frame of small-diameter tubing and independent suspension to all four wheels. The engine was a 2½-litre 4-cylinder, designed and built in their own factory and took a lot of knowledge from the 8-cylinder Mercedes-Benz M196 in that it was canted over almost horizontally, thus giving a very low bonnet line, and the valve operation was 'desmodromic' with two camshafts and induction was by Hilborn injection. As the design had been started in 1958 the layout had the engine at the front, on conventional 'old-fashioned' lines. By 1960 even the Scuderia Ferrari was going 'rear-engine' and the Scarab was obsolete before it even started in a race.

Chuck Daigh with the Scarab in the Inter-Continental Formula International Trophy at Silverstone in May 1961. The race was run in torrential rain. (T. C. March)

Reventlow and Chuck Daigh ran the two cars built in the early season races in Europe, but before mid-season they knew they were wasting their time and money, so the whole team was packed up and returned home to California, wiser but sadder. Two cars had been built, and a third was partly built, but was never completed.

In 1960 Chuck Daigh brought one of the Scarab cars back to England to take part in the short-lived Inter-Continental Formula, with the engine enlarged to 3 litres, but it was no more successful than it had been in Grand Prix racing as a 2½-litre.

In recent years Tom Wheatcroft has acquired the half-finished third car for his Donington Racing Car Museum. It was finished as a static exhibition for the collection, static by reason of the fact that there is no Scarab engine available for it. Even so, it is a car that is worthy of study and it is a pity it was too late. In the context of the 250F Maserati and the DBR4 Aston Martin, the Scarab might well have held its own with a bit of race experience. As it was, it was a very expensive 'folly'.

Semmence Special

Built in 1936 this homemade special had a very workmanlike air about it and was so well proportioned for its day that it could be taken for a factory produced racing car. It was constructed by Humphrey Whitfield-Semmence in his own garage-cum-workshop and was based on Frazer Nash components, which included the chassis frame and the 4-speed chain transmission. The engine was a 2-litre A.C. 6-cylinder of 'vintage' parentage, the single overhead camshaft cylinder head being fed by three S.U. carburettors. The slim single-seater bodywork was reminiscent of a contemporary E.R.A. and, in fact, the whole conception of the Semmence Special was that of the 'poor man's' E.R.A., even the 6-cylinder exhaust system being E.R.A.-like.

Whitfield-Semmence used the car in speed trials, mostly on the South Coast at places like Lewes, Brighton, Southsea and Poole, and it was very well known up to 1939. After the war it re-appeared in new hands, including those of Leslie Hawthorn, father of the lad who was to become World Champion Grand Prix driver in 1958. It passed through various hands on the club racing scene and was a regular competitor in sprints and hill-climbs, even aspiring to some circuit racing in VSCC events. It is still in the Vintage/Historic world, and has always been powered by an A.C. Six engine; considering how many hands it has been through it has stayed remarkably much as it was originally built, which must be a testament to Whitfield-Semmence getting the whole concept right at the start. 'Genuine '

H. Whitfield-Semmence with the 2-litre A.C.-powered Semmence Special in 1938. (The Geoffrey Goddard Collection)

Sunbeam

The Sunbeam company of Wolverhampton were racing as long ago as 1912, in the 3-litre Coupe de l'Auto, and one of these cars still exists, living in the National Motor Museum at Beaulieu and having the occasional outing. The 1914 Tourist

Trophy Sunbeams, although blatant copies of the previous year's Peugeot racing cars, were well made and sound cars. Of the team of three cars, two are still in fine health and are exercised regularly in VSCC events, while the third car has recently returned to the United Kingdom from New Zealand, where it has been since the early 1920s.

The Sunbeam firm was very busy during the 1914–18 War on government military projects and aero-engine building, and by 1919 they had new racing cars ready for the Indianapolis 500 Mile race. Racing activity was prolific for a number of years and their 3-litre straight-eight racing car won the 1922 Tourist Trophy, while new 2-litre 4-cylinder cars were running in the French Grand Prix. All the racing Sunbeams from 1914 onwards were of the classic Peugeot design with twin overhead camshafts and were beautifully made pure racing engines of very high standard.

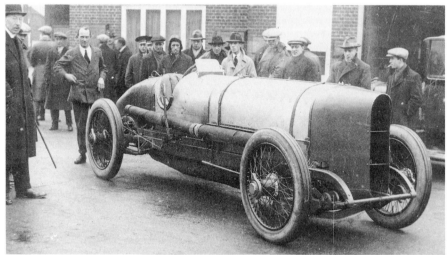

The 350 hp V-12 Sunbeam in the Brooklands Paddock. (The Geoffrey Goddard Collection)

In 1923 the Grand Prix Sunbeams had new 6-cylinder twin-cam engines and it was one of these that put the name Sunbeam on the Grand Prix map when Henry Segrave won the French Grand Prix at Tours. The following year the Grand Prix Sunbeams were supercharged, and though the 1923 design has gone down in history, the 1924 cars were the pinnacle of Sunbeam Grand Prix design.

Fortunately there are still a number of survivors from the great days of the Sunbeam, to show the sporting world today that we were very strong in Grand Prix racing in the early days. One of the 1922 cars has survived intact over the years and can still be seen in action in VSCC events, still looking every inch a pure 'toolroom' factory racing car. Another was retrieved from obscurity and 'resurrected' to perfection and is still prominent in VSCC circles. The three 1923 cars were dismantled by the racing department, including the French Grand Prix winner, and they formed the basis of the 1924 factory team cars, and one of these supercharged 6-cylinder 2-litre cars is still very much 'as it was in the beginning'.

When the Sunbeam firm withdrew from Grand Prix racing the supercharged 6-cylinder cars were sold to private owners and all three proved very successful in national racing events, from hill-climbs and sand-racing to Outer Circuit racing at the Brooklands track. No. 1 was raced by May Cunliffe and then went to Ireland,

The 1924 Sunbeam Grand Prix team at the French race at Lyon with, left to right, Resta, Segrave and Guinness. (The Geoffrey Goddard Collection)

The 4-litre Sunbeam V–12 'Tiger' with Sir Malcolm Campbell at the wheel at Brooklands. (The Geoffrey Goddard Collection)

where it was still racing into the late 1930s, No. 2 was raced up to 1932 by E. L. Bouts, and No. 3 was raced by Kaye Don and others and became a legend of Brooklands racing and record breaking and was known as 'The Cub.' Over the years No. 1 deteriorated and became altered in many ways, but the bones still remain in Northern Ireland in the Ulster Transport Museum; No. 2 was made into a road-going sports car, with a Rolls-Royce engine replacing the blown Grand Prix engine, and is still safely in the hands of a VSCC member, while No. 3 never suffered the fate of deterioration or modification and is safely in the National Motor Museum, complete and very 'Genuine'. It comes out for an airing on special occasions, and the sound of that 63-year-old supercharged engine is glorious, even by today's standards.

In addition to their Grand Prix activities, Sunbeam also went wholeheartedly into the realms of record-breaking and were continual contenders for the Land

Speed Record. For this they built cars powered by aero engines and also a very advanced 4-litre car that was, in effect, a large Grand Prix car. In the Beaulieu Museum is the 350 hp V-12 aero-engined record car that was driven by Malcolm Campbell, and the twin-engined record car with which Henry Segrave was the first man to exceed 200 mph.

The car with which Segrave had put the record up to 151.31 mph in 1926 was of pure Grand Prix design, with a 4-litre V-12 supercharged engine that was, in effect, a direct descendant from the 1924 Grand Prix engine, with each bank of six cylinders having its own supercharger. Two of these cars were built to race in non-Formula events and the record breaking was something of an extra. Kaye Don raced them at Brooklands and eventually Malcolm Campbell bought them and had them extensively redesigned and rebuilt by Thomson & Taylor. The rebuild included new chassis frames, new front axles, hydraulic brakes, and the fitting of Armstrong Siddeley pre-selector gearboxes, so that they became virtually Campbell–Sunbeam Specials, though still essentially the 4-litre V-12 Sunbeams. In their heyday they had been named 'Tiger' and 'Tigress' (hence the 2-litre of Kaye Don being name 'The Cub'), and 'Tiger' was still being raced up to 1937.

After the war 'Tiger' joined the VSCC ranks and has only stopped racing to undergo major rebuilds and overhauls, and it goes as well today, if not better, than ever it did. 'Tigress' was cannibalized in the thirties to keep 'Tiger' racing, though the main components were always around. She has now been 'resurrected' to join her illustrious brother in the Historic world.

Talbot-Darracq

When the French Darracq company joined the Sunbeam-Talbot combine to form Sunbeam-Talbot-Darracq, or S.T.D. as it became known, the cars from the Suresnes factory in Paris became known as Talbot-Darracq. The racing programme of the combine continued unabated, even though there were times when it was difficult to distinguish between a Talbot-Darracq racing car and a Sunbeam racing car.

The 1926 Talbot-Darracq Straight-eight 1½-litre cars at Brooklands.

For the 1926–7 Grand Prix Formula of 1½ litres, Darracq produced a totally new and individual model. It had a supercharged straight-eight engine with two overhead camshafts in true racing tradition, and the chassis frame was a steel trellis construction. The cars were very low, with the driver sitting offset alongside the transmission, and very pronounced sloping radiators were used. Although they were a match in design for anything in the Grand Prix world at the time they never performed outstandingly and were overshadowed by the 1½-litre Delage cars. Their racing life was curtailed when S.T.D. withdrew from racing in 1927 and although two of them survived, they never made a serious mark in racing in the way the Delage cars did.

Anthony Powys-Lybbe, the English amateur driver, had one resurrected in 1937 without much success, and it later went to Australia, where it still lives. Another was developed by 'Gigi' Platé in Italy and was still racing in 'voiturette' events as late as 1947, but was equally unsuccessful. Recently the remains of a third car were discovered in South Africa.

Talbot-Lago

When the S.T.D. combine closed down in the mid-1930s the French Talbot-Darracq firm was taken over by Anthony Lago, and he restarted a very busy racing programme. France was encouraging sports car racing in 1936 and new Darracq sports/racing cars appeared with 4-litre 6-cylinder pushrod ohv engines. They were very successful and in 1938 they could be used in Grand Prix racing, running without road equipment and with the passenger seat covered over. This encouraged Tony Lago to turn his thoughts to building Grand Prix cars, based on his sports car components.

The 6-cylinder engine had inclined overhead valves operated by long and short pushrods and rockers, from a single crankcase-mounted camshaft, and breathed through three downdraught carburettors. A Wilson pre-selector gearbox was used and the rather primitive channel-steel chassis had independent front suspension by solid wishbones and a transverse leaf-spring, while the rear axle was rigid and mounted on half-elliptic leaf-springs. After building two single-seaters with the driver sitting offset alongside the transmission, Lago built a pure single-seater with the driver sitting centrally. This *Monoplace* appeared very briefly in 1939, at the French Grand Prix.

After the war the *Monoplace* was raced extensively and led to the introduction of a new car, the T26C in 1948 for the new Formula for unsupercharged 4½-litre engines and supercharged 1½-litre engines. A new engine was designed and built, using inclined overhead valves operated by short pushrods and rockers from a camshaft on each side of the cylinder block, on the Riley Nine principle, and the capacity was taken up to the full 4½ litres. A Wilson pre-selector gearbox was still used, and behind it a gear train stepped the drive to the right so that the driver could sit low alongside it, and be centrally placed in the chassis.

A production series of these ready-to-race Talbot-Lagos was put in hand and though they were rather big cars, and not very fast, they were remarkably reliable and economical on fuel. They could run through a 300-mile Grand Prix without stopping and often beat their faster supercharged 1½-litre rivals by this fact alone, taking the lead when the thirstier cars had to stop for fuel.

Raymond Mays with the 1939 Monoplace *Talbot-Lago in the French Grand Prix at Reims.*
(Louis Klementaski)

The Talbot-Lago of Pierre Levegh in the 1950 International Trophy at Silverstone.
(T. C. March)

    The factory continued development of the T26C until 1950, supporting private owners as well as a factory team. These vintage-style single-seaters made up a large proportion of the Grand Prix grids of the day, but could never be considered front-line Grand Prix contenders. Most of the 14 single-seaters have survived intact, though some were converted into two-seater sports cars. They joined the factory sports car versions that were made, using the same components as the single-seaters. Many are sitting quietly in museums and others can be seen in action in Historic racing, though the tortoise-and-hare syndrome no longer applies in the short sprint affairs of the Historic scene. All that a Talbot-Lago owner can do today is to enjoy the satisfaction of driving an Historic car, which is a friendly, nice old vehicle, but not a natural winner. For this reason there has been no incentive to build 'Facsimiles' and create new history. The Talbot-Lago scene is a quiet, serene one, in the manner in which the T26C used to go racing when it was new.

Acknowledgements to *Talbot–Des Talbot-Darracq aux Talbot-Lago* by Alain Spitz, Éditions E.P.A., France.

Trossi-Monaco

Augusto Monaco was an Italian special builder who created quite a successful hill-climb car with his friend Enrico Nardi, but he then had ambitions to build a Grand Prix car. With Giulio Aymini he designed a revolutionary racing car in the mid-thirties with a view to Grand Prix racing. He got the Fiat company interested in the design and they actually built the engine, which itself was revolutionary enough as we shall see. Before the project was really under way Fiat pulled out and Monaco was lucky to arouse the interest of the rich and noble Alfa Romeo racing driver Count Carlo Felice Trossi. The extensive workshops at Count Trossi's family castle at Biella in northern Italy were made available and the car was completed in 1935.

The chassis frame was built on aircraft lines from small-diameter tubing and was what became known in later years as a 'space-frame'. The engine was a 'way-out' as was the chassis, for its time, and was a 4-litre twin-piston two-stroke with eight double cylinders arranged on a circular crankcase, to give in effect a 16-cylinder radial layout. Behind the cylinders were two Zoller superchargers feeding the rear row of cylinders, with the exhaust ports out of the front cylinders, the combustion chambers being single units to each pair of cylinders, which were heavily finned, relying on air cooling. This remarkable power unit was mounted on the front of the 'space-frame' so that the car looked like an aeroplane without wings. Behind the engine and under the two superchargers was the 4-speed gearbox and differential unit from which universally-jointed shafts drove the front wheels. Suspension was independent to all four wheels, and with no propeller-shaft running down the centre of the car the driver could sit very low within the chassis frame, the top rails being nearly at shoulder height. Everything was covered by a simple alloy-sheet body made in sections and attached as panels as on an aircraft.

Its paper specification for 1935 sounded most unlikely for a serious Grand Prix contender, as it would today; 4-litre, air-cooled, 16-cylinder, radial double-piston, supercharged two-stroke with front-wheel drive, all-independent suspension and tubular 'space-frame' chassis. It sounded as though it wouldn't work, and it didn't! The car ran on test at Monza prior to the 1935 Italian GP and was thought to have reached 150 mph, but the designer had been talking optimistically of 190 mph,

The radial-engined Trossi Special now displayed in the Biscaretti Museum in Turin.

which is what it would have had to achieve to match the Mercedes-Benz and Auto Union Grand Prix cars of the time. After that one test session the car went back to the Trossi castle, whether to the workshops or the dungeons was never revealed, but whatever happened it survived.

After the Count's death his widow presented the car to the Biscaretti Museum in Turin, where it can be seen on display today.

The Trossi-Monaco comes in that category of racing cars known as 'did it really happen'. Fortunately it has survived in its original form and makes an interesting study for students of Grand Prix car design.

'Genuine '

Vanwall

When the B.R.M. project was launched in 1945 Tony Vandervell was a keen supporter and offered the facilities of V.P. Products, his shell-bearing factory at Acton, for manufacturing processes as well as the supply of bearings for the V-16 engine. It was not long before he became disenchanted with the progress and design and management behind the B.R.M. and withdrew his support in order to run his own team. After racing Ferrari cars, V.P. Products produced their own car for Grand Prix racing and it was called the Vanwall, a name derived from Vandervell and Thinwall, the trade name of V.P. Bearings.

Starting with a single car in 1954 Tony Vandervell built up one of the most powerful Grand Prix teams that Britain had ever seen. After two troublesome learning years in 1955 and 1956, the team began to make its mark in 1957, winning their first World Championship event at Aintree, the British Grand Prix, following up with victories at Pescara and Monza. Among the teams they were beating were Gordini, Maserati, Ferrari and B.R.M. In 1958 they dominated the Grand Prix scene, winning six of the nine World Championship events they entered, running a team of three cars driven by Stirling Moss, Tony Brooks and Stuart Lewis-Evans, a remarkably talented trio of British drivers who often filled the front row of the grid. That year Stirling Moss missed the Drivers' Championship by a single point, but the Vanwell team easily won the Manufacturer's Championship.

As far as Tony Vandervell was concerned it was 'mission completed' and he

Peter Collins with the original 'Vanwall Special' in the 1954 Italian Grand Prix at Monza.
(LAT)

Stirling Moss with his Vanwall in the pits during practice for the 1957 Syracuse Grand Prix. Tony Vandervell stands alongside the cockpit. (Motor)

Tony Brooks with the short-nose Vanwall that he drove into second place at Monaco in 1957. (Motor)

closed down his powerful racing team and for the next three years ran a single experimental car in one or two events. Throughout the life of the team his cars were the property of V.P. Products and he never lent one to anybody, or sold one, and the only drivers to race the Vanwalls were those chosen by Tony himself, and employed as professional works drivers.

When Tony Vandervell died in 1967 his bearings empire was taken over by the GKN Group, the Acton establishment was closed down and everything was concentrated at the Maidenhead factory at which the VP bearings were being produced. During the life of the team Vandervell had insisted that no more than four were kept assembled, even though he had built a total of 12 cars; this was to avoid trouble with the tax man, as the racing team was part and parcel of the Research & Development department of VP Products. Everything was moved down to Maidenhead and the four cars kept on the books were the 4½-litre Ferrari Thin Wall Special, which had set the team on the road to success, VW9, which was a 1957 Formula 1 car, polished and painted as a 'Show Car' with a perspex engine cover, VW10, which was a 1958 car, and was kept in running order as a 'demonstration' model, and finally VW14, the last car built by the team, which was an experimental rear-engined car.

In recent years a 'new' Vanwall was built with the blessing of the management of GKN-Vandervell. It used up accumulated spare parts built on to a newly built chassis frame and body. While it was not one of the famous 1958 team cars, it was a true 'replica' built by some of the men who had built the original cars, though it was made outside the Maidenhead factory. It raced in a few Historic events and then joined the famous cars in the Donington Collection of single-seaters.

After caring for and maintaining the racing heritage of Tony Vandervell for nearly 20 years, GKN-Vandervell decided it had been faithful to his memory long enough and the word went round that the four cars and all the spares and bits and pieces would be put up for auction. However, before that happened the whole lot was sold to Tom Wheatcroft by private treaty, to join his vast collection of Grand Prix cars at Donington Park. Everything was packed up and transported to Donington Park in 1986, including the Thin Wall Special, the rear-engined VW14 and the two front-engined Vanwalls, cars VW9 and VW10.

History

Vanwall Special	1954 Prototype car	Crashed at the Spanish Grand Prix. Broken up.

Vanwall VW1	1955 team car	These four car were driven by Mike Hawthorn, Ken Wharton, Harry Schell and Desmond Titterington. No cars survived as they were broken up to form the 1956 team.
Vanwall VW2	1955 team car	
Vanwall VW3	1955 team car	
Vanwall VW4	1955 team car	

Vanwall VW1/56	1956 team car	These four cars were driven by Stirling Moss, Harry Schell, Maurice Trintignant, Mike Hawthorn, Colin Chapman, Froilan Gonzalez and Piero Taruffi. VW2 won the International Trophy at Silverstone. No cars survived as they were used to build the first four 1957 cars.
Vanwall VW2/56	1956 team car	
Vanwall VW3/56	1956 team car	
Vanwall VW4/56	1956 team car	

Vanwall VW1	1957 team car	These ten cars formed the pool from which four cars were kept fully assembled and used by Stirling Moss, Tony Brooks, Roy Salvadori and Stuart Lewis-Evans during the 1957 season. VW4 won the British GP, VW5 won the Pescara GP and the Italian GP. VW6 was the experimental streamlined car, not raced, and then became a normal 1957 car. VW8 and VW9 had 'lightweight' chassis frames, though VW9 was never completed, nor was VW2
Vanwall VW2	1957 team car	
Vanwall VW3	1957 team car	
Vanwall VW4	1957 team car	
Vanwall VW5	1957 team car	
Vanwall VW6	1957 team car	
Vanwall VW7	1957 team car	
Vanwall VW8	1957 team car	
Vanwall VW9	1957 team car	
Vanwall VW10	1957 team car	

The Vanwall in 1958 with wire-spoke front and cast magnesium rear wheels. Stirling Moss is seen on his way to victory in the Dutch Grand Prix at Zandvoort. (Motor)

The ten 1957 cars continued into the 1958 season, being rebuilt and modified in many ways. VW1, VW2, VW3 and VW8 were never assembled during 1958, but acted as spare parts for the team. VW4, VW5, VW6, VW7, VW9 and VW10 provided the team cars for Moss, Brooks and Lewis-Evans. VW4 won the German GP, but was destroyed in a crash at the Moroccan GP. VW5 won the Belgian GP, Italian GP and Moroccan GP, VW10 won the Dutch GP.

Vanwall VW11	Experimental car built in 1960 using the basic components of VW5, which had already been heavily modified in 1959. Called the 'low-line' car.
VW12 (officially designated VWL12)	A Lotus 18 chassis number 901, which had a Vanwall engine installed in the rear for experimental purposes. Used for testing, but never raced.
VW13	Not built.
VW14	Last car built. Rear-engined car for Inter-Continental Formula racing in 1961, driven by Jack Brabham and John Surtees.

Acknowledgements to *Vanwall* by Denis Jenkinson and Cyril Posthumus, Patrick Stephens Ltd.

Vauxhall T.T.

In 1922 Vauxhall Motors did a strange thing – they produced a team of sophisticated and advance racing cars with 3-litre engines just as the International Formula had been reduced to 2 litres! The RAC were organizing their Tourist Trophy race in the Isle of Man to the 3-litre rules of 1920–21, but all the other important International events were to be run to the new 2-litre Formula. Whether the Vauxhall management thought the RAC were going to influence the rest of Europe, or whether they had not appreciated the International situation is not clear. Alternatively they may have started the project with a view to racing in 1920 and 1921 and merely taken too long to get the cars finished, which has happened since in British racing car building.

Whatever the reason, the cars were very interesting when they appeared in the Isle of Man, even though they were not successful. The 3-litre engine had been designed by H. R. Ricardo and was a 4-cylinder with four valves per cylinder, two overhead camshafts gear driven from the front of the crankshaft and operating the valves, which were at 90 degrees, through small rockers. The flywheel was mounted at the centre of the fully roller-bearing crankshaft, within the crankcase, and though the ignition was by a single central sparking plug, there was provision on each side for two alternative positions.

After their one important outing these Vauxhalls could then only be used in club events and they raced on the Brooklands banked track, with some success, at sand races such as Southport and in hill-climbs. At Brooklands they proved capable of speeds around 115 mph and it seemed clear that had they been ready in 1921 they could have given a good account of themselves in the French GP against the contemporary 3-litre Ballot and Duesenberg opposition.

As they reached the end of their life in Club racing they became absorbed into

The 1922 Tourist Trophy Vauxhall with Humphrey Cook at the wheel in the paddock at Brooklands. (The Geoffrey Goddard Collection)

various specials, the Raymond Mays Villiers Supercharged special being the most famous, and many of the bits and pieces survived. In recent years a VSCC member has reconstructed a car to the 1922 specification, but while it cannot be considered to be a 'Genuine' car, it certainly is an 'Authentic Re-creation' if you can have such a thing!

Vauxhall-Villiers

Raymond Mays developed this car from one of the original 1922 T.T. Vauxhall 3-litre cars. With the assistance of Amherst Villiers and Peter Berthon it became one of the most potent sprint and hill-climb cars in the early 1930s. Villiers specialized in supercharging and engine development, and applied one of his own superchargers to the 3-litre engine, mounted vertically in front of the block and driven by bevel gears from the nose of the crankshaft. Deep side-plates were bolted to the chassis frame to increase its stiffness in bending and special hubs to take twin rear wheels were fitted to the differential-less rear axle.

As the power output was increased to nearly double its original output, a larger radiator core was needed and the car lost its traditional fluted Vauxhall radiator and received a functional squared-off wide core. Testing was frequently carried out on the open road, and during its life it carried at least two different registration numbers. The two-seater body layout was retained, enabling a passenger to be carried, and Peter Berthon often rode up Shelsley Walsh with Raymond Mays.

During its life with Villiers and Mays it was given a variety of names, Vauxhall-Villiers, Villiers-Vauxhall Supercharged Special or Villiers Supercharged. When Mays moved on to Rileys and E.R.A. development, the Vauxhall-Villiers was sold and S. E. Cummings had a very successful season with it in 1936 before passing it

Raymond Mays at the wheel of the Villiers-Vauxhall with which he competed so successfully in hill climbs between 1928 and 1933. (The Geoffrey Goddard Collection)

The Amherst Villiers-supercharged engine of the Villiers-Vauxhall. (The Geoffrey Goddard Collection)

on. It then went through hands that thought to improve on the work of Mays and Villiers. The engine/gearbox unit was removed and put into a Type 54 Bugatti chassis, but that proved to be a failure and the original 1936 Vauxhall-Villiers more or less disappeared into various component parts.

It was resurrected after the war in somewhat similar form, but had independent front suspension added, but as Historic cars began to come into vogue it was totally rebuilt on one of the original T. T. Vauxhall chassis frames and put into the form it was in 1929. In this form it has been active in the VSCC for many years, and is still an exciting performer, even being driven on the road to Shelsley Walsh at times.

'Authentic '

Veritas

Ernst Loof had been in the factory B.M.W. racing department up to the outbreak of war, learning a lot about the racing Type 328 B.M.W.s. When the war finished and it seemed that B.M.W. AG were never going to get back on their feet in motor racing, Ernst started his own small company expressly for getting involved with the reestablishment of motor racing in Germany and Europe.

His first move was to offer to 'race prepare' 328 B.M.W. sports cars, and then to convert them into pure racing cars. Formula 2 had been created for International racing, with a capacity limit of 2 litres without superchargers, so the 328 B.M.W. engine was tailor-made for the job. The alloy-head 6-cylinder B.M.W. engine, with its ingenious hemispherical combustion chamber with inclined valves operated by pushrods from a single crankcase-mounted camshaft, had already been giving 130 bhp in special factory form in 1940, so was.a strong contender for Formula 2.

Ernst Loof had formed the Veritas company and offered a service for building Formula 2 cars, provided the customer could produce a 328 B.M.W. sports car to start with. As work progressed Loof altered the chassis of the B.M.W. extensively and eventually built his own chassis in its entirety. The next step involved the engine, for he had reached the limit of development of the basic 328 B.M.W. engine, and it was not long before this was replaced by a 6-cylinder of similar proportions, but having a single overhead camshaft along the centre of the head. This pure Veritas engine was manufactured for Veritas by the Heinkel firm and appeared in Veritas sports cars as well as single-seaters.

In the early days of the firm, relations with France were naturally a little sensitive, even though French motor racing people were interested in the cars, so a number of Veritas cars that went to France carried the name Meteor.

The single-seater Veritas was a good private-owner car, but it was no match for

The offset single-seater Veritas driven by Toni Ulmen in the 1952 International Trophy at Silverstone. (T. C. March)

Ferrari and Maserati opposition. When Formula 2 ended in 1953 Ernst Loof had expanded his firm into a manufacturer of quite civilized road cars, in coupé and cabriolet form, but it was a very specialized market and the cars were expensive to build. As the German industry got back on its feet the future for small firms like Veritas was bleak and with the new Formula 1 racing being beyond his means, Loof closed down Veritas and rejoined the B.M.W. Research and Development Department.